CW00695364

june's accidental knowledge

June Lobb

Copyright © 2013 June Lobb

First published 2013

All rights reserved

Designed by June Lobb
Allsorts Publishing ®

Printed by Quine & Cubbon

For my Mother

Acknowledgement

Recounting how I came by my "accidental knowledge" covers a time span of over 30 years. In that time, I have met so many different people, too numerous to mention all by name, both good and bad, though at times there was good to be found in the bad (just not enough of it). I would like to thank you all for your contributions to my greater understanding of life and all it's myriad aspects.

Special thanks go to my family for putting up with me, and to my editors Sylvia and Kenneth Knight for all their painstaking work and encouragement.

Most of all, and for the rest of my life I will be grateful to Doctor E. M. Abrahamson and A.W. Pezet for the book *Body, Mind and Sugar* and to J. I. Rodale, for introducing me to it via J.I. Rodale's *Health Treasury*.

Introduction

Maybe, as a child, my grandmother read me too many fairy stories with happy endings. I grew up with the idea that I was going to have a happy life. But my mother left my father when I was six months old, because her parents considered him unsuitable. Some years later, she married again, to someone more unsuitable. Disastrous.

After that, I was so unsettled that I was happy to marry when I was 17. My life would be perfect. I would make sure that it was perfect. After all, one only has oneself to blame if their life isn't perfect, don't they?

My marriage survived twelve years. I had met my husband to be when I was 15. When I decided to end it, I didn't know that I was already in the early stages of a breakdown, which happened after I left. After that the real chaos of my life began, and with it a huge learning curve. My health had never been good, and I had had little work experience. I had worked on a farm for a while after I left school, having only managed to pass my Art 'O' level and failed everything else.

Still, I decided to have a go at everything, and if I failed at least I would have tried. So I tried my hand at property renovation, worked as a rep for a travel agency, as a waitress, as a barmaid, as a secretary, drove a butchers van delivering meat, worked on a market stall, in a newsagent's (at one point having to fix a wreck of a car that I bought, before I could drive it away), in a market garden, stacked shelves in a supermarket, worked in a gent's outfitters (I had really wanted to work in a smart ladies dress shop), married an Indian gentleman, and started up an Indian restaurant (that turned out to be a very expensive cookery lesson), worked in an open-all-hours shop, in a tailor's shop, doing alterations, in a filling station, opened a Health Food shop.

Unwittingly, and without my realising it at the time; upon leaving my husband and having a breakdown, or, one might say, having a breakdown and leaving my husband (since the two seem interwoven), I had enrolled into the "school of hard knocks". And although I felt utterly miserable at the time, there can be no argument, other than that the breakdown that I had was one of the best things that ever happened to me. It was the beginning of my traumatic learning of life; an awakening that helped me to see life through different eyes, in all its harsh reality.

Finally, I became a self-employed gardener, work which I came to realise I had a vocation for. I had grown up with people who had an interest in gardening, I loved it all of it, the scientific side, the creative side, even the weeding and clearing.

My gardening work would regularly require me to visit the local "recycling centre", in order to drop off "green waste" for my customers, and a perk of this exercise would be that I would be able to have a look around and see what had been dropped off for recycling.

In 2002, I picked up a book that was going to change my life forever, although I did not realise this at the time. J.I. Rodale's Health Treasury, published in 1962.

There was a short section in it on asthma, just five pages. The clear and very positive message was that asthma could be controlled by diet, and that it is triggered by diet in the first place, and linked to low blood sugar conditions.

I found this hard to believe, but since there was a recommended dietary guide in the book, I decided that I had nothing to lose by trying it. To my utter amazement, the asthma attacks stopped. It was marvellous. I felt so different, but my doctor was sceptical. Actually, it was more than that. He wasn't even interested. However, my interest was awakened, and I became obsessed with "the diet". It was quite complicated, and I decided to revise it. I have a deep rooted interest in nutrition and I had a lot of health problems. I could use myself as a guinea pig, and take notice of any changes to my various ailments.

I wrote a simple-to-understand self-help booklet, the format being (I hoped), simple enough for anybody who was able to read to understand. This was completed in October 2006, four years after finding the book "J.I.Rodale's Health Treasury" in the tip. I did not manage to get my booklet published, and was later to be so relieved that I didn't, as it was only in my 10th year of study, that I was shocked to find that a vital clue that previous research had revealed, had either been missed or misunderstood.

My current doctor is, and has been very supportive. He commented some time ago that most research studies are carried out over a relatively short period of time. It would not have been financially viable to carry out a study, as I have done, over a period of ten years - 24 hours a day -7 days a week - 365 days a year.

My book charts my journey, and the "accidental knowledge" that I have gathered along the way. What I have gained is priceless beyond measure. I now live an uncomplicated, rewarding and healthy life.

June Lobb. March 2013

june's accidental knowledge

Chapter 1

Many many years ago, in what seems like a former life, a life disconnected to the one I live now coincidences occurred of which I took little or no notice at the time. I was married and living on the Isle of Man with my husband Peter and our son Douglas.

When I first met Peter, it was March 1967. He had a car, or rather a mini pick-up, a vehicle nonetheless.We would go for drives into the countryside,sometimes up to the Lake District. From time to time, but not on every outing, Peter would pull into the side of the road and say he just had to stop for a little while. He said he was having what he described as a 'funny do'. He would just be quiet for a very short time and then, when he felt alright, we would set off again. It never occurred to me to feel any kind of alarm. I trusted him completely and he seemed to be in control of the situation, plus I was very young at the time - 15, Peter was 17.

I never gave much thought to Peter's 'funny do's' as he called them, until after we had moved to the Isle of Man. One morning, we were in the kitchen and Peter was sitting at the kitchen table eating breakfast. I must have moved away to get or move something when I became aware of a slight whimpering noise coming from the direction of the table. I turned round to see Peter making tiny shuffling movements with his feet and small involuntary movements with his hands, accompanied by the low whimpering noise. It lasted only seconds. When it stopped, I said, "Peter, have you just had one of your 'funny do's'? "He said he thought that he had. I told him that it looked like he was having a fit. Such was his nature though, that he was instantly on the defensive and denied that he could possibly have had a fit. I was to find, as the years went by, that he would not discuss or accept anything that he did not feel comfortable with, regardless of the consequences.

After the episode in the kitchen, when I witnessed the first seizure, I became acutely aware of them. He no longer pulled off the road for a few minutes quiet recovery, but carried on driving. How he didn't have, or cause, an accident is little short of a miracle.Time and time again, I would reach over and keep the car on course until he regained control. A seizure could occur at any time, without warning. More than once, he had one on a motorway. By now, I was thoroughly alarmed and wanted him to take medical advice but he didn't want to admit there was a problem. The worry of the seizures now chewed at me constantly and I nagged him to go and see the doctor. Finally, he went and was referred to the hospital for brain scans, to see if there was an underlying reason for the fits.

Amazingly, the doctor did not suggest that he should stop driving. The scans all showed normal brain function.

Chapter 2

Peter worked for a firm that serviced and repaired heavy plant machinery. The firm also hired out machinery with a driver, if a driver was required. Peter had had training to drive the machinery. He would also have to deliver and collect machinery that was either going out on hire or being returned. Sometimes, during the school holidays, he would call to see if Douglas wanted to go with him for the ride and if he wasn't playing with his friends, he always went. Peter's seizures were getting worse now, but I seemed to be the only one for whom the alarm bells were ringing.

During a half term break, I heard the landrover and trailer pull up outside the bungalow. I was in the kitchen, making bread and had just added the yeast mixture to the flour and was mixing it in. Douglas had been playing in the back garden and had also heard the landrover. He came in to see if his father had called to pick him up, to go for a ride. Peter was going to collect a dumper. He asked if I would like to go with them. It was a lovely day, so I thought, "why not?", washed my hands and put a damp cloth over the dough. We all got into the landrover. There was a long seat in the front. Douglas sat between Peter and myself.

There were times in those long past days when we did, albeit briefly, feel like a happy little family unit. We arrived at a junction in Douglas called 'The Brown Bobby', the right hand road leading down a hill towards the promenade. At that time, I think that there were only two sets of traffic lights on the Island which probably helped what was about to happen, because just as we cleared the brow of the hill, Peter began to have a seizure. Douglas was sitting in between us. Peter started the, by now, characteristic whimpering, his hands making involuntary movements on the steering wheel. His right foot went hard down on the accelerator, his left foot shuffled about on the floor. I suppose it's an automatic panic reaction, I shouted,"Peter, Peter, what are you doing? Brake! Brake!", as I leaned over to hold the steering wheel and guide the speeding vehicle down the narrow road, avoiding other vehicles. Of course he couldn't hear me. We careered over the crossroads at the bottom of Athol Street, hurtling down the hill towards a zebra crossing and the bus station. All I could think of was keeping the vehicle on a straight course, desperately hoping that no-one would step out into the road, that a car would not pull out of a side road. Just before we reached the roundabout, at the bottom of the hill, Peter's whimpering stopped. His hands grasped the steering wheel again. He took his foot off the accelerator, applied it to the brake and changed down a gear. He was back in control.

I said, "You've just had a fit. We could have caused an accident. Somebody could have been killed!"

He didn't say anything. Just fit continued driving. The dumper was collected, myself and Douglas were deposited back at the bungalow. Douglas went to play. I dealt with the by now mountainous bowl of dough.

My mother was aware of the seizures. We were due to have another consultation with the specialist. My mother made the suggestion that maybe Peter's over use of the nasal sprays could be affecting his brain (he was using sprays for nasal congestion when I met him. He used them constantly, carrying one with him at all times and panicking if he ran out.). I said I would mention this to the Consultant. I went in with Peter to hear the outcome of the latest brain scan. Nothing untoward had been found. There was no explanation for the seizures. I asked the Consultant if I could have a word with him in private. He agreed and I suppose Peter must have gone and waited outside. I broached the subject of the nasal sprays and asked if the long term use could possibly be affecting his brain. The Consultant was quite confident that there was absolutely no possibility of the nasal spray causing fits. Grasping at straws, I asked the Consultant if he would ask Peter to stop using the spray for a while, just to satisfy me, since Peter was disinclined to take any notice of anything I said. He said he would do. He asked me to ask Peter to come back in. He went in and I sat outside and waited. He came out and we went home. He made no mention of the sprays but dutifully stopped using them. Within a month he had stopped having fits. I can't remember if the nasal congestion remained a problem. It can't have done because I am sure that I would have remembered.

Chapter 3

All sorts of things are going on in a person's life at any one time. Children succumb to childhood illnesses. Adults have adult problems. Cars break down or are changed. People go to work, change their jobs, lose their jobs, move house. The seasons change. All manner of things are happening all the time. My grandfather died suddenly. He dropped dead in front of me. He would never have wanted to linger on, in failing health, but my grandmother and I got a terrible shock. It takes time to re-adjust after such a loss but, eventually, she decided to move and we gradually adopted a new routine. She moved to Port Erin and on Friday mornings she would catch a bus over to where we lived at Ballasalla and we would go grocery shopping together, coming back in time to have lunch with Peter and Douglas. After lunch, I would go and pay Peter's wages into the bank. Then I would take my grandmother home. This week was a little bit different, though. It was March and the daffodils were in bloom. A neighbour had asked if she could go with us. A friend of her's was away on holiday and had told her that she could help herself to daffodils from the garden. The garden was at Colby and meant going back to Port Erin on a different route to the one I usually took.

After lunch, Douglas went back to school. We collected my neighbour. I called at the bank but when I came out, it had completely slipped my mind that we were supposed to be going to Port Erin via Colby. I got back in the car and, without thinking, began to pull out of the car park, as if to go along the coast road, past the airport. My neighbour quickly reminded me that we were going to go through Colby. A vague feeling of uncertainty came over me. I had totally forgotten about going to pick the daffodils. I backed the car a little so that I could now pull out of the bank car park in the opposite direction. It was a mild, dry day. I drove out of Ballasalla towards the crossroads at Cross Four Ways, along the short straight before the dip and slight bend in the road, by what used to be Roy Gelling's farm, up a slight rise and then along another short straight. I doubt we were doing thirty miles an hour. Ahead was a blind bend to the right. As we got nearer, a tractor and trailer load of bales appeared, just clearing the corner as we approached it. Then out of the blue, a van appeared, overtaking the tractor on the bend, at high speed. Odd, the way everything seemed to slow down. There was nowhere to go. The tractor and trailer on one side and wall and hedge on the other. I remember wondering briefly whether I had time to put the car into reverse. But, instead, I said "He's going to hit us!" and he did, knocking the car back down the road. Everything stopped. I struggled to get out of the car. The impact had pushed the wing over the door. The two young men in the van had got out and were standing by it. I asked them what the Hell they thought they were doing and was told that they were driving very fast. When they were actually on the bend and saw the tractor and trailer, they knew they couldn't brake in time, to avoid running into the back of the trailer and decided to take a chance and overtake it and hope that nothing was coming the other way. In other words, they simply decided to overtake a long vehicle on a completely blind bend. I went back to the car. My grandmother was sitting awkwardly, there was blood coming out of her nose and ears. She said that she couldn't move. My neighbour in the back was unhurt and went to phone for an ambulance and also, to let Peter know what had happened. He arrived shortly after the ambulance.

He looked at the car and said, "You've ruined my car!". Then after a moments pause, he asked if I was alright. His reactions to situations were always totally inappropriate. It was disheartening.

Many years later, I would reflect on this experience when I decided to write down my thoughts on coincidence and what I thought might be happening.

Chapter 4

The rest of the day began to feel surreal. I went with my grandmother to the hospital. I was sure that she would be on her feet again in a few hours. We arrived in Casualty (as it was then). My grandmother was taken into a room at the back. I waited, feeling lost and shocked. Hours passed. It went dark. No-one came to see if I was alright. Eventually, a doctor came out from the back of the waiting area. He came up to me and asked if I was the driver of the car. I said I was. He said that she (she, being my grandmother), would never walk again and that she would probably die, that I might as well go home but I could go and see her before I went. Of course I went to see her. She was suspended in a sort of hammock. I can't remember what I said, other than that I would be back the next day. I went back into the waiting area. It was now that I started to feel weepy. I had not brought any money with me and I did not know how I was going to get home. I must have been looking lost, as a nurse came up to me and asked if I was alright. She was going off duty and took me home, though I can't actually remember getting home, or the events of the evening. It never occurred to me that it was odd that Peter hadn't come to the hospital. Though years later with the benefit of hindsight and knowledge, I would understand that there were possible explanations for his bizarre behaviour.

Traumatic and difficult months followed, and my grandmother died, roughly eight months later, in the November. Unfortunately, rather than being supportive during this time, Peter became increasingly demanding and unreasonable. I had begun to feel as though I was living in a waking nightmare. Nothing made sense. Peter was not the kind of man that I could talk to and I began to feel detached. We went to spend Christmas with his parents, but my feeling of isolation and detachment was slowly growing all the time. Back home, in January, I went through the motions of doing what I had always done. Peter's inclination to nag and complain had always been a trial to cope with. His bouts of bullying Douglas were unbearable. I was feeling switched off.

My mother had left my father when I was only a few months old. She had married him secretly and her parents had not been invited to the wedding. The fact that she was an only child and adored by her father did not make it the most auspicious of starts. When they did meet him, it would appear that he was considered not good enough for their precious daughter and they set about persuading her to leave him. Having successfully engineered that, they then whisked her away to Hampshire where she went to Art School and lived in lodgings and they took charge of me. I was never to see my father again and, being so young when my mother left, I had no recollection of him. I was unaware of any of this until I was much older. My mother finally met someone else and wanted to remarry. Her parents opposed the union at first but later relented and my mother remarried. She then wanted her daughter back but since I was coming up to 4½ by this time, we had missed the vital early bonding. I did not feel comfortable with my mother, I didn't like my stepfather and I missed my grandparents. As it turned out, the marriage was pretty much doomed from the start. I felt it had been very damaging for me. I didn't want Douglas to go through anything like that. I mention this, at this point, because I had decided from the start that I did not want to be like my mother and have a broken marriage. However, it is all too easy to judge other people's actions and as I was about to find out, there is far more to this life than meets the eye.

Through January, I had some kind of mental shift and the emotional environment that was once familiar and gave me a sense of belonging, despite the discord, was no longer there. For Peter, I felt I had no feelings whatsoever and was merely fulfilling a house keeping role. I began to have vision disturbances. I couldn't look at patterns (for instance the patterns on the carpets or curtaining), soon I began to have difficulty looking at any kind of patterns without them separating and lifting, making me feel as though the space I was in was getting smaller. I would try focusing on blank surfaces to try to ease my mind. Nobody seemed to show even the slightest concern for me and my loss. I began to wonder if I would be better off on my own. I wouldn't have to cope with the daily complaining and nagging and Douglas would no longer be bullied and tormented by his father. Although again, as I was later to find out, emotional damage had been done.

Chapter 5

The last straw didn't actually arrive, as such, after a tension or how one would expect a last straw might be triggered. It was, in fact me, having another mental shift. Years later, I would read about post traumatic stress and wonder if this had something to do with my problem. It happened at the end of the day, when Peter came in from work. Washing his hands in the kitchen sink, he said, "What's fer tea?"

I was standing at the back of the kitchen, watching him. I felt like I was a long way away and, as I stood there, what I can only describe as a grey gauze screen appeared to slowly come down between us like the curtain at the end of a scene in a play. I suppose it was an hallucination. But I could see Peter on the other side of it, and I felt that this particular chapter in my life had come to an end. As I mentioned previously I never had been able to talk to him. Had I been able to, things may have turned out differently. (Years later, by chance, I was to become aware of a condition called Alexithymia. I was also to gain an understanding of autism). After that, the rest of the day and the evening progressed as normal. We ate our evening meal. I washed up. The evening passed. The next day, though, I did not feel any different and I began to worry about how to tell Peter how I felt. His usual response to anything I said would be, "Ay lass, you're talking rubbish."

A few days later, I said, "I need to talk to you."

His reply, "What's up lass?"

Mine, "Peter, we need to separate, I can no longer cope."

This, for him, was an absolute bombshell and I think for the first time in our marriage he was truly awake. He said he knew how badly he had treated me and that he was sorry and that he would do anything if only I would stay. Sadly, his mental shift occurred after I had gone past the point of no return and he had not got the capacity to help the situation. He did suggest seeing a marriage guidance counsellor, but I was just past it.

My emotional state worsened and where ever I looked I could see patterns separating. I also began to suffer from severe headaches. It didn't occur to me to visit a doctor or confide in Peter how terrible I was feeling. I used to suffer from asthma which Peter had concluded I did on purpose. I also suffered from overwhelming bouts of tiredness and depression. For most of the time we had been married I had been on pretty much a starvation diet, in order to stay slim.

Peter couldn't bear the thought of my getting heavy. Every now and again, I would relax and over eat and put weight on. This would horrify him and I would be back to my calorie counting. The trouble was, I was not naturally slim and did not know how to be slim, without constantly dieting. Also, I was expected to produce the best of meals. I liked food. It was difficult.

A few weeks passed. I was very weepy and used an attack of bronchitis as a reason to move into the spare room, saying that I didn't want to disturb his sleep with my coughing and wheezing. I can't remember when our financial arrangements changed but they did and although he did give me a little money I subsidised this, making and selling soft toys. The reality of what I had set in motion gave me cause for concern. What I should have done or tried to do, I didn't do.

Instead, I insisted that the bungalow be put up for sale. Later, it occurred to me that I should probably have tried to buy him out, but the place no longer felt like home. I couldn't cope with all the separating patterns and I just wanted to be somewhere else. I wanted peace and harmony. Someone did make an offer on the property but Peter did not want to accept it as he thought we could get more. When an offer was finally accepted, it was much lower than the one that had been declined.

Chapter 6

I had always been in love with the idea of buying an old place and doing it up. It was during that year of mine and Peter's estrangement that I found, for sale, a derelict cottage in Castletown. At this point I had no idea that I was in the preliminary stages of a breakdown. I did have some money tied up in various small investments provided by my grandparents. They were producing very small dividends or none at all and I felt that the money would be more useful invested in providing a new home for Douglas and myself. With the sale of the shares, I managed to scrape enough together to buy the cottage and also to get Peter to agree to the sale of the bungalow on the lower offer. I also had to agree to him having a certain amount out and me paying the costs and not claiming any maintenance. At this point I would have agreed to almost anything, in order to get away.

While all this was going on, I was trying to find a job that would somehow fit in with being at home, as much as possible, for Douglas, and I was having no luck. Then, one day, my neighbour, with whom I had always been close, asked me if I was still looking for a job. Her sister worked on the Dublin telephone exchange and, at that time, there was no direct line to the Isle of Man, so all calls were routed through the operator. One day, her sister had been putting calls through for a travel agent for whom she put calls through on a regular basis, when he asked if she knew anyone on the Island who wanted a job. She said that she would mention it to her sister who lived on the island. My neighbour mentioned this to me and, less than a week later, I met the man in question and was given the job.

The work involved the office in Dublin calling me with a list of bookings to ring through locally. I also had to vet hotels, give my opinion of the standard offered, negotiate tariffs and deal with any difficulties that arose. Perfect. I could work from home and the pay was quite good. All I had to do now was get my new home ready. A happier life was waiting for me. Or so I thought.

I took Douglas to see the cottage. It was very delapidated. The old plaster was falling off the walls. There was an outside toilet, not working. There was a cold water tap, over a shallow ware sink in the tiny lean to kitchen, and the back door was patched up with bits of boards. A little garden, which backed on to the seashore, was a tangle of overgrowth. The front of it was not rendered and had many layers of lime wash coating the stonework. This was much weathered and now had the appearance of so many oyster shells, but I was so desperate for some peace and quiet that I would have happily moved into it, just as it was. However, poor Douglas was very upset and near to tears and worried what his friends might think. I think, at that moment, he would have preferred us to remain as the dysfunctional little family that we were. I really didn't want him to be any more unhappy than he was already. (The road to hell being paved with good intentions). So I started getting quotes from building firms for renovations. I did have a definite idea of what I wanted to do, but the builder that I ended up with had his own ideas.

"Leave it to me love. We are used to doing up cottage properties" or, "I wouldn't recommend that. A better way to do it would be ….." All the "better ways to do it", caused the cost to spiral ever higher.

Sometimes I would go over in an afternoon to see how things were progressing. More than once I came across the workmen sitting, enjoying a fire of redundant timber, drinking tea and playing cards. The renovation that I ended up with was awful, had cost more than I could afford and I hated it. I realised that I should not have been talked out of my original ideas and vowed never to use a building firm again.

Another very difficult and strained year passed and Peter and I parted in April of the following year. The bungalow had been sold and my cottage was in a reasonable state to move into. I thought I would feel better and that life would settle down. It did, for a while. But I had launched myself into this new independence with no formal qualifications and very little experience of work. Peter hadn't wanted me to go out to work and so I had contented myself looking after my little family. I began to make a mess of the new life. My mental state had not settled down and then a string of misfortunes tipped the balance and I had a breakdown. It started with the travel agents that I had been working for having a crisis and my income and financial security came to an abrupt halt. Then, a man who had decided that he was madly in love with me decided that he wasn't after all. I foolishly clung to him and tried to talk him round. He had, for a while at least, been kind and had made me laugh. Humour was something that poor Peter had been unable to cope with. He had problems with sadness too, in fact with any kind of emotional issue. It was the end of the year and on Dec 21st, the winter solstice, a strange little anonymous letter arrived for me.

Nowadays, I would take no notice of anything like that and would probably just throw it away, but in my vulnerable emotional state, I felt confused. When I took the card, or rather folded piece of paper, out of the envelope, I had felt puzzled. The front of the paper had crudely drawn images that pointed to it being sent by the man who had rejected me (though he denied any knowledge of it). On opening it, a hypnotic orange eye stared out at me. A mystic, who lived a few doors away, informed me that it was the eye of Horus and that someone had put the 'evil eye' on me.

Not having taken much interest in the ancient Egyptians, I did not question the mystic's word and began to worry that some harm was going to be inflicted on me. (Odd that, at that time, no-one else seemed any the wiser either, and so I remained ignorant of the fact that the Eye of Horus is, in fact, a symbol of protection, royal power and wealth!). As the days went by, my anxiety was turning into paranoia. Now, on top of everything else, I was developing a persecution complex. I began to feel I was dealing with forces of darkness. I went to the doctor with my anxieties and was given sedatives. (Will the reader please take note here that at no point did any doctor enquire about my eating habits or diet).

I wasn't sleeping and had been unsuccessfully trying to find work. I began to drink heavily, hoping that the drink and the tranquillisers would help me to sleep. At night, when I did manage to sleep, I had nightmares and would dream that I was fighting with the devil. Or I would be wakened by the sound of the outside doors being opened and then being slammed shut, and the sound of heavy feet on the stairs, then my bed being surrounded by presences of people, standing unseen. I would say "Go away! I am not afraid of you". Strangely enough, when I said this the dream or halucination, or whatever it was, would end.

My mental state was going from bad to worse. I had now been referred to a psychiatrist. No-one seemed to think that there was very much wrong with me. I was prescribed stronger tranquillisers. I was totally losing touch with reality. I had developed an obsession with the eye in the anonymous note I received. I saw eyes everywhere and thought that the forces of darkness were watching my movements and communicating about me, by telepathy. I was genuinely expecting to be attacked. My headaches now were mind-numbingly painfull. I felt as though the top of my head had been removed and my brain was being prodded with sharp sticks. On top of the tranquillisers and heavy drinking, I was now taking massive doses of painkillers.

Chapter 7

The winter dragged on. Everything was depressing, the weather, the news (the Faulklands war was in progress). Even the music in the charts was sad. David Essex sang, 'It was only a winter's day ...'

Odd people used to turn up at the cottage and then pour out all their problems. I looked out at what was to be my paradise view and saw grey rocks, grey sea and grey sky. I was beginning to lose all hope of finding a reasonable job. February came. I was still tormented with the paranoia. I was convinced that it was just a matter of time before the 'attack' would take place. I also felt as though I was disappearing down a vortex in the labyrinth of my mind and that I was rapidly moving backwards, away from what was the present time. My days were now spent in a state of perpetual high anxiety. Meanwhile, I made meals, took the dog for walks and appeared outwardly as though nothing was wrong. One of my friends suggested that I might find it comforting if I went to church and found a faith. However I had never been able to quite 'get' religion and so I could not imagine it affording me any consolation; Besides which, the mystic who lived nearby had told me that people who practised witchcraft went to church, then took communion, only to get the holy bread and then use it in their satanic rituals. Since I was convinced that it was people who practised witchcraft that were going to attack me, the church would be the very last place I would be going. It was also suggested that I talk to someone in the Samaritans, but, by now, I was so paranoid that I was convinced that 'they' would have people planted everywhere, noting my decline. I was now feeling that the 'attack' was imminent and would happen at any time. What, in fact, was imminent and about to happen at any time was me having a mental breakdown, brought on, I would say, from living in a depressed state for a long time.

February 4th 1983 I felt that all the signs were in place and today 'it' was going to happen. The day got off to the wierdest start imaginable. Even if I had not gone nuts, I would have wondered about it. I went out to the back garden. Birds were sitting all around the walls but not in any kind of threatening way. It was more as though they had some sort of shared concern for me. Some comfort in that. I looked up and saw the clouds briefly form a jovial smiling face. Just as I was about to relax slightly, the smiling face was replaced by a dark, brooding, angry one. This made me feel nervous and heightened my paranoia. I went inside and arranged to go with one of my friends to visit another friend. On the way, noticed that a lot of people seemed to have their windows open, the sort of windows that swung out from hinges on the top of the window frame, which seemed odd for February. I became convinced that the witches were signalling each other and were closing in. We arrived at the friend's house. In her living room, I looked out of her window and noticed windows open in what I thought was an empty house. I became convinced that 'they' were in that house and that 'they' were closing in. I was wound up to breaking point. Meanwhile my friends were chatting about ordinary things. I, however, was thinking of ways to escape. I decided to go to the bathroom. Once in there, I locked the door. Now I had decided that my friends were 'in on it', as well, and that I had been brought there for a reason. I decided to escape through the bathroom window. At this point, my friend's husband had come home, and as I had been in the bathroom some considerable time, they were starting to wonder about me. I was asked if I was alright. I didn't answer but panicked and swept everything off the bathroom windowsill, intending to escape. Before I managed that however, my friend's husband broke down the bathroom door and grabbed me before I could get out through the window. He carried me into the living room. Terrified, I crawled behind a chair and refused to come out. Minutes passed. The tension in me built to breaking point and I had a screaming fit. My poor friends! They rang for a doctor. The doctor arrived. He looked the exact double of a man who I had been told was a practising witch. He went. A social worker arrived who looked the exact double of my long deceased stepfather. I braced myself for what I believed was going to be a terrifying fate. It was decided that I should be taken under Section to the local mental hospital. My dear friend offered to come with me. A car arrived, with a nurse, and I sat in the back between my friend and the nurse. They both held my hands but I was convinced that they were going to deliver me to 'them'.

We arrived at the hospital and I was taken to a secure wing. At the sight of a little room with bars on the window, I decided I had to make a break for it, but was quickly overpowered by three nurses and taken into the room. They then held me down and gave me a sedative jab. They went out and locked the door. A piece of wood could be slid across the window from the outside. From time to time, this would slide back and someone would peer in at me. There was absolutely nil reassurance in any way, shape or form in those first few terrifying hours.

Chapter 8

So nothing happened. Meals were brought in, I was kept sedated and given sleeping pills. My friends came to see me. My mother took a few days off from her teaching in England and came to see me. It was decided that she would take Douglas back to stay with her until I felt better. I saw the psychiatrist that I had been seeing. I asked him if I was schizophrenic. He was incredibly kind and reassuring and said that I was not. He said that there was nothing wrong with me but that I had been having a very troubled time over a long period and had just cracked in the end.

As it turned out, I was only in hospital for 10 days. I went home. Nothing had changed outwardly. Still no job. Very little money. However I had changed. I understood quite clearly that the crisis had been all in my mind and that it was unreal. There were no dark forces of evil at work. One of my friends visiting me had said that the experience would make me stronger. I emerged a total atheist, believing in neither God nor the Devil and vowed that nothing and no-one would ever put me through anything like that ever again.

Douglas was now with my mother and wrote to me almost every day. This was starting to worry me, although it had only been a couple of weeks. I didn't want history repeating itself with my mother feeling that she had to take charge of my child. Although the circumstances were different,there was a worrying parallel.

I was still taking tranquillisers. I had also been prescribed sleeping pills and for the first time in many years, I enjoyed guaranteed sleep every night. I was seeing the psychiatrist once a week for counselling and although he was very kind, I did not feel the visits were benefitting me as all I did was go over the past and sit and cry. Finally I decided to stop going and I let him know how I felt. I always had the option to go back if I couldn't cope. I also stopped taking the tranquillisers. I did continue to have anxiety attacks but they passed, they decreased in frequency and were not as severe. They were not part of any paranoia so I lived with them. I now had the benefit of clearer thinking. I had cleared my mind of a lot of medieval beliefs and superstitions and no longer felt threatened.

I went over to my mothers for a short break and to bring Douglas home. This was still only March though and already the year seemed very long. When we got back Douglas went back to school. I struggled to make ends meet and thought about work. I had eleven pounds a week single parent family allowance, plus a further ten pounds that my mother sent. People were extraordinarily kind. The butchers always had a bag of useful, meaty bones that I could use to make soup and broth. Plus there would be trimmings of meat that I would use to make stews. Douglas, during this time was an absolute tower of strength. Each day seemed like a week. I still didn't have much "get up and go". Despite everything I would tackle in the future, leaving that first marriage would always be the most difficult thing I had ever done.

Easter was approaching. We decided to go and spend a few days with my mother and two brothers, my half brothers from her second marriage, quite a bit younger than me, but we all got on reasonably well. On the boat coming home, I bumped into one of the hotel managers that I had met when I had been riding somewhat higher, working for the travel agents as a rep. He asked how I was. I said that I had had a breakdown and was out of work. He invited me to go and work the summer season as a waitress in his hotel. He said that he would pay a stamp for me and that at the end of the season I would be able to claim the dole. It sounded like a hand up. So I thanked him and arranged to call and see him the following week. One of the reasons that I hadn't been able to claim the dole or any benefit when I ceased working for the travel agency was that they had been paying me cash until they made me a bonafide member of staff, which, as the reader will be aware, didn't happen.

Anyway, I went over to the hotel in Port Erin to discuss my employment. It felt like a come down. I was given a tour of the kitchen and the dining room and a general idea of my duties. Plus, I was told, outworkers are not allowed any food. Only the workers living in were provided with meals. All tips were to be placed in the tip box and at the end of the season I would be given a substantial amount as a thankyou. I was then taken to a room where the "uniforms" were kept. From a crumpled pile in a cupboard, a creased black dress with white collar and sleeve trims was handed to me. It smelt strongly of the previous season's wearer and the previous season's food. I took it home and washed it. I was to start work the next week, helping to get the place ready for the first visitors, early season Irish cheap package holidays.

My mother sent some money and I bought a cheap car. I parked it on the carpark opposite the cottage. Overnight, the wing mirrors were broken off and someone had run a sharp object along the length of the car, damaging the paintwork. How is it that some people have nothing else to do with their time other than be destructive?

Chapter 9

Monday morning came round. Douglas went to school and I left soon after, in some old clothes, to go to my new job, getting the hotel ready for opening. I was nervous. I got to Port Erin and parked outside the hotel. The company owned two hotels on either side of a roadway that led into a cul-de-sac. I went into the hotel where I had had my interview and found my now "employer". He told me that I was to start across the road in the other hotel and that he would come with me and introduce me to the other members of staff. We walked into a room full of bustle and bright light and noise. I was almost immediately overtaken by an anxiety attack. Too much activity, too much noise and too much bright light. My heart was racing and I felt nervy. I would liked to have run away, but the anxiety attacks were different now. I was fully aware that there was nothing here to harm me. I told myself that I was a stronger person. I was introduced to the other members of staff, mostly Irish and come to the Island to work for the summer season. The only "locals" were myself and the two chefs. I realised that I still had some problem with my vision. Maybe predictably, when I happened to speak to anyone, I noticed that their eyes seemed unnaturally bright and emphasised. Bright lights were too bright. But apart from that, I survived. Everybody was friendly and helpful. There didn't seem to be any hierarchy. We worked until the kitchen and dining room were ready for use. We were to do the kitchen and dining room in the other hotel the following day.

The other hotel was slightly smarter. The dining room was less like a canteen. It took most of the day to get it ready. Checking cutlery, checking crockery, cleaning shelves. All the staff were already making jokes about their employer. One of the chefs told me not to put all my tips in the tip box as he had worked there the previous season and only had a minute payout at the end.

"Put some in," he said, "but keep most of it".

The first guests were due to arrive the following Saturday. I had to be there at 7.45 a.m. Those first few weeks were exhausting. The hotel did half board, so after the breakfast things were cleared away, I went home for the middle part of the day, then back, to do the evening meals. The season wore on. Everything got busier. Staff began to walk out and at the peak of the season we were reduced to three waitresses, myself and two others.

Finally it all came to an end. Uniforms were handed back. No doubt, to be tossed into the same cupboard, unwashed, until the next season. I was handed my last pay packet and a brown envelope with my tips for the season. I checked my pay packet for the record of contributions. Nothing there. So I went to enquire and was told that he didn't pay a stamp, just cash. So that was that, and no hope of any dole. I looked in my tip envelope. £5. The last day at the hotel was the last day of the week and marked the end of the summer season. It was the middle of September.

Chapter 10

I had got to know a few of the neighbours along the little terrace of cottages where I lived. There was a very nice couple next door who had been wonderfully kind while I had been at my lowest ebb. Next door to them was a single retired gentleman who was eager to tell me about himself. He had served in the Indian army and had been highly decorated with an, O.B.E. C.B.E. and M.B.E. Although how true that was I will never know. He was very open about his past and said he had always enjoyed business ventures. However, he had, at one point, been involved in a fraudulent enterprise and had got caught. He ended up going to prison for five years. During that time, his second marriage had ended, and when he came out of prison he took refuge in the Isle of Man. The cottage that he was living in was owned by some friends of his.

His experience in prison had affected him. He still wanted to be involved in business, so he worked from home, occupying himself with company management and formation, but also acting like a modern day Robin Hood for people who were running small businesses and who had got behind with their accounts and tax returns and had no-one to turn to. Sometimes I would go and have a cup of tea with him and hear about his adventures. I would also spend time with the couple next door. They were all nice, steady people. I was back to looking for work, applying for positions that were advertised in the local paper. I got as far as interviews but was never successful in getting full time, rewarding employment. I hadn't got much experience of anything other than being a housewife, a rep., having a breakdown and working one season as a waitress. I had worked on a farm after I left school.

Money was becoming a big worry again and winter was approaching. The lady who lived next door to me said that she had noticed in the local paper, one of the nearby pubs advertising for a part-time barmaid. I had a bit of a problem with that, inasmuch as I didn't much care for pubs and had only ever been in one on a few occasions. My step-father had been an alcoholic and it had left it's mark on me, with me having an aversion to "pub culture". On the other hand, I realised I was never going to get idyllic employment so I rang up and arranged to go and see the landlord. I was given the job straight away and was due to start the following Friday. I felt frightened, but by this time I was no longer having anxiety attacks. It was not just the new work to get used to, but the fact that I would be serving alcohol and I was not sure what to expect. I was to work six days a week from 3.30 p.m to 7.30 p.m.

I duly turned up on the Friday and was introduced to the departing barmaid (who was very popular and leaving to go to university), and who would show me what to do. On Fridays, the local factory closed early for the weekend and this pub was the favourite place to go, the builders also used to come in and then there were the regulars. By 4 p.m the place was buzzing. The departing barmaid had been drenched with the soda syphon and the atmosphere was lunatic. People that had been in the bar since lunchtime were drunk, the factory workers were getting drunk. Some people were argumentative, some were morose, women were chatting up men, men were chatting up women, some were stealing other people's drinks when they weren't looking. The phone would ring with wives looking for their husbands who, in turn would instruct whoever answered the phone to say that, "No, they weren't there."

I was bombarded with information, asked questions, given advice. The tills were not computerised then and everything had to be totted up mentally. So, in that one mad afternoon I had to learn how to pull pints, change kegs, in short get the hang of all of it. And I had no choice since there was no financial safety net. It did get better though. The landlord decided to take on another barmaid to work part of the afternoon with me. She did a different shift and would start at 12.00 and finish at 4.30 p.m. The first of the evening staff would come in then, with someone else replacing me when I left at 7.30 p.m. The lady that came to work with me had spent much of her life in South Africa and was very glamorous, plus she had a marvellous sense of humour. So we did have an absolutely hilarious time for a while.

Meanwhile the pub work, on it's own, wasn't really enough for Douglas and myself to live on. But as luck would have it, the retired gentleman next door but one decided to rent a nearby office and start up again in business proper. He asked me if I would like to go and work for him as his secretary/p.a. I could work mornings 9.30 – 12.30 p.m. Things were starting to fall into place again. I took a sigh of relief and enrolled on a typing course at night school.

Tom really was a delight to work for. He had taken on some rooms on the top floor of a building with the very proper address of Parliament Square. He had his office and he put me in an adjoining office of my own. He would go into work at 6.30 a.m and I would start at 9.30. He would have put a heater on in my room and was quite happy for me to bring the collie Oliver with me. I was always greeted with tea and biscuits on arrival and Oliver soon understood where the biscuits were kept.

The business of helping people with their chaotic accounts and tax arrears got very busy. Desperate people would arrive at the office with carrier bags full of invoices, sometimes three or four year's worth. These would all have to be sorted out into date order and then written up into double entry ledgers. This was one of my jobs. Douglas was able to earn a bit of pocket money doing this as well and soon got the hang of sorting through invoices and getting them ready for me to write up and tot up the columns. In those days, or maybe it was just Tom, but if a column was out by even a penny, it had to be found. Maybe that was something to do with Tom having been in prison, I don't know. Tom would then analyse the written up accounts and deal with the tax office.

After the uncomfortable and bumpy first year in our cottage, some feeling of normality was seeping back into our lives. Douglas had had to change schools but he had managed to make new friends. His childhood was more normal. He went fishing, he swam in the sea with his friends. He did not have to spell " P-L-E-A-S-E M-A-Y I L-E-A-V-E T-H-E T-A-B-L-E-" over and over again after a meal, and then be told not to cry if he got upset, or sent to his room if it was not a school day. I used to challenge Peter's unreasonable behaviour and this would cause further upset. There had seemed to be no way to resolve these terrible tensions. I had, though, on more than one occasion, asked Peter what was wrong with him, and he had replied that he didn't know. So things had calmed down considerably. But nothing stays settled for long.

Something went wrong between the landlord and his wife at the pub and she left him and went back to Ireland. He turned to drink and already being a heavy drinker, things got bad. Eventually he and his wife came to some sort of compromise and it was decided that the pub, which was freehold, would be sold and he would go and join his wife in Ireland.

The pub was bought by a brewery who appointed a manager. The staff were to be kept on. It was alright initially. The manager and his wife seemed to be working hard at making a good impression. She worked like a slave in the kitchen, he got drunk with the locals. After a few weeks he suggested that I might be better off giving up the office work and working a few more hours in the pub. He told me that I would then be able to claim F.I.S.(Family Income Supplement) and this might make life a bit easier for me. At the time it did sound like a good idea and I had to tell Tom that I was going to leave. He was really upset, angry even, and said that I was to stay until I had found a replacement. It was surprisingly easy to find a replacement. I suppose in a small place where everybody knows everybody else's business, all the in's and out's, Tom's little business would be known. I found a lady a bit older than me with better office skills who would, in fact, probably, be much better than me. Tom was happy and I left to work longer hours in the pub.

It was after I went to work solely in the pub that the landlord made his first pass at me, or rather grope. He decided to grab me one day and ask if I "fucked".

I said "No, I don't," pushed him away and went into the kitchen where I thought I would be safe among the other staff.

He followed me in, however, and began some sneaky touching

"Stop that!" I said

"Stop what? "he said

"Stop bloody groping!" I said and went off to the public bar which was now open.

A couple were waiting to be served. She ordered a gin and tonic "NO ice" and he had whisky and water "NO ice" I had just put their drinks down when the landlord arrived in the bar.

Straight away he said to me "June! Put ice in those drinks!"

He then got rebuked by the customers who said that they hadn't wanted ice. So now, he was not just frustrated and cross, he was also humiliated. I was to pay a pretty high price for that. The wages were paid on Friday evenings. That Friday everybody got paid but me. By Sunday I was practically begging for my wages, it didn't occur to me to report him to his employers for misconduct. I couldn't deal with this kind of tormenting, it was my husband all over again or my stepfather. It was just another bully.

After, I finished work I went to the pub across the road and asked if they needed any staff. The landlord asked when I could start.

I said "Now, if you like."

I started the next day. It was a different type of pub, rough really, but the landlord was not a drunkard and did not abuse his staff. Having made the move, I could no longer claim F.I.S. The butchers who had been so kind while I was ill needed a van driver to deliver meat around the hotels in Douglas, plus a few deliveries to make on the way back. So I became a part time van driver as well. The van was a bit rickety. The driver's seat was not fixed down on the inside, which meant that when I went around a right hand bend, the seat lifted off the floor and I was leaning against the door until I was on the straight road again. The brakes were a bit suspect as well. Anyway, all went along reasonably well for a while. The pub crowd were more earthy than in the first bar. But odd things happened nonetheless. There were people who went to work, went to the pub from work and then just went home to sleep. Their children were practically raised on the pub doorstep. To me, it was still a different and unreal world. One couple in particular, who spent every evening in the bar and who weren't in the least unpleasant, were the cause of great amusement one evening. She had been sent some money for her birthday and didn't want her husband to know. She also wanted a toasted sandwich. I was to make one and then hand it to her very quietly so that her husband didn't notice. This was possible as her husband was deep in conversation at the other end of the bar. However, no sooner was the cellophane wrapping off the sandwich than her husband paused in his conversation and sniffed the aroma. Now, people would buy snacks all evening and nothing untoward would happen. He, however, linked this smell with his wife having a sneaky snack, as she was. He put down his drink, looked over, saw the sandwich in his wife's hand and rushed over and tried to grab it from her. She held on grimly and so there they were, fighting over a sandwich, to the amusement of the onlookers. I had never seen anything like it. They both ended up with bits of it and then went back to their respective ends of the bar, as though nothing had happened.

Chapter 11

Weeks passed, I continued working part-time at the pub, delivered meat at the weekends, I earned a little extra money helping to run a market stall in the summer. One of my friends ran the bar and kitchen in the local flying club and I would stand in occasionally for her doing a lunchtime session while she did food hygiene courses at the local College of Further Education. Working in the pub I was getting used to the drinkers and the pub culture and had begun to think, maybe it's not so bad after all. I had got involved with one of the builders that frequented the bar at teatimes. I was unaware of the rumour circulating that I was well off and would be a good catch!

The truth was quite the opposite. I did own my cottage. Apart from that, I was really struggling to make ends meet. I was running up an overdraft at the bank which was becoming unmanageable. Then something happened that made me decide to move right away to another part of the Island and start afresh. I was delivering meat in Douglas and had parked the van outside a hotel (This was in 1985, very little crime here then). I left the keys in the ignition and took the tray of meat from the back of the van, carrying it through to the kitchen where I spent a few minutes talking to the staff. When I came out again,there was no sign of the van. My stomach turned over a I imagined the worst. Then I noticed a small group of people gathered further down the hill. They were looking at my van which had rolled back down the hill and into the side of a parked car. But for the car that it had run into, the van would have dropped into the hotel basement outside which the car was parked. How very embarrassing! I walked down the hill to the van and explained that it was mine. I left a note on the windscreen of the damaged car, giving the butcher's name and phone number plus an explanation and an apology. Then, watched by the bystanders, I got into the van, drove off, and carried on with my round.

When I got back to Castletown, the butchers had already had a phone call from the owner of the car and their insurance was to pay for the repair.

"Didn't you leave it in gear, as well as having the handbrake on?" My employer asked.

I hadn't and I felt really bad about my mistake. After a few weeks, the butcher told me that the car that had been damaged by the van running into it had not only had a new door, but a complete respray. I felt worse, and the bank was getting twitchy about my overdraft and I couldn't seem to earn enough. I decided to put the cottage up for sale.

I still liked the idea of fixing up a property and I had my builder friend now living with me. I had noticed a disused chapel on a country road and made enquiries regarding the owner. I was told that it had been for sale at one time but now just stood empty. I thought what a lovely place it would be to live in and so wrote to the owner, expressing my interest. I received a reply saying that if I would like to make a reasonable offer, it would be considered. I wrote back with my offer and waited expectantly. No reply came. Meanwhile I put the cottage up for sale. The third person to see it decided to buy it, at my asking price. I began to look for a property to renovate. There was still no reply from the owner of the chapel, so I assumed that my offer wasn't high enough and since I couldn't afford to offer any more,

I decided not to pursue it any further. Everything seemed to be out of my price range. If I could afford a property, I wouldn't have enough money left to pay for the renovations. Time was passing. I looked at an end terrace cottage on the shipyard in Ramsey. It was quite remarkable with the inside constructed entirely of wood. Old fashioned tongue and groove boards formed all the partitions. It had a cold tap and an outside toilet and a little front and also a back garden. It had been for sale for quite a while and I made an offer a thousand pounds below the asking price. This was accepted, but curiously enough, the day that I signed the contract for the purchase of the cottage, I came home to find a letter from the owner of the chapel, accepting the offer I had made some months before. I couldn't afford to do both so I had to write back and thank him and let him know that his acceptance had come just one day too late for me to follow it up.

The purchase on the cottage was duly completed. It was late spring and I bought a tent for us to live in, whilst we worked on fixing it up. My mother was friendly with a farmer and his wife and family in Ramsey, and they very kindly fenced off a corner of a field for us to pitch the tent in. The farm dairy was just across the road and we were invited to help ourselves to buckets of hot water for washing. There was an outside toilet in the farmyard that we could use.

Douglas was in his last year in school (he had never really settled down after all the upsets, the motor accident, my leaving his father and my subsequent breakdown), and did not want to stay on, especially if it meant moving to another school. We moved into the tent. It was quite large and had two bedrooms and extra space for a table and chairs and an awning for cooking under. I was feeling happier and optimistic again. We still had Oliver the collie and I suddenly had a hankering for a cocker spaniel. No sooner had I been possessed of this need than I noticed an ad in the paper for cocker spaniel puppies for sale. I rang up and was told that they were two weeks old and would be ready to leave their mother at ten weeks. We went over to see them. I chose one that was "mis-marked", she had white freckles on her nose, and so could not be classed as a pure pedigree. In another eight weeks we estimated that we would be moving into the cottage, so the timing was quite good.

Meanwhile, life continued in the tent and on the building site. The inside of the cottage had been completely stripped out. A planning application to install a bathroom had been submitted and passed and we had worked out a plan for the inside of the cottage. We changed the position of the staircase to accommodate the bathroom. The cottage at Castletown had been the same layout as this one, just basically two up and two down and no bathroom. A narrow bathroom had been installed but it had no window, and I always thought that there must have been a better way to do it. This time, we applied for the installation of an extra window and took roughly a third off the size of the front bedroom for the bathroom. The bedroom was still a nice size and so was the bathroom and the other bedroom was a double. It was very satisfying getting it to work. Downstairs we made open plan.

It was whilst everything was still in a state of upheaval, with floorboards up and plumbing and rewiring and plastering going on, that I received a phone call from the woman with the cocker spaniel puppies which were now six weeks old. She said that she had to go away and that if I still wanted the puppy I would have to go and get her that weekend or an alternative home would have to be found. We went down at the weekend to collect her. I didn't know much about very small puppies and how long they should stay with their mothers and she did seem very young. I handed over the £90 in cash and we set off back to Ramsey. The schools had broken up for the summer holidays and we were all still living in the tent. Sometimes Douglas would have a friend to stay for the weekend. It was all quite an adventure.

We called the puppy Dusty since she was always covered in dust. There had been no choice but to take her along to work with us. She would wander around among the workmen and fall down gaps in the floorboards. Oliver, the collie, did not like her at all, and kept looking at me in a sort of reproachful way, as if he was asking "Why, have you done this?"

Worse still for him, as the puppy was missing her mother, when he lay down, she would go and curl up with him. His reaction to this would be to give a long suffering sigh, get up and go and lie down somewhere else. As soon as he moved, the puppy would look round sleepily and then go and curl up with him again. And so it went on. He took a long time to get used to her. In the end, he gave in as she never gave up.

Chapter 12

Across the road from the property we were working on was a larger derelict Victorian house. I thought that it looked very sad and wondered if the person who owned it might want to sell it. By this time, I had got to know the town surveyor quite well as he came to inspect and pass our various stages of progress on the renovation of the cottage. On one of his visits, I asked about the other property. He said anyone who took it on and made it habitable would be doing the Commissioners a favour, as they would soon have to enforce a closing order. This meant that the Commissioners would undertake the basic repairs to make the property safe. The owner would then have to foot the bill. I contacted the owner. He was quite keen to sell his house and we agreed a price, which was very low, but probably appropriate as the place was in a very poor state. Meanwhile we finished work on the first cottage and the surveyor issued a habitation certificate. All the proceeds from the sale of the cottage in Castletown and been used up in the just completed renovation and a fair bit had also gone over the bar in various pubs and on cigarettes.

This was beginning to worry me a bit, but not enough to stop me pursuing the goal of the next house. I went to the bank at Castletown to see if it would be possible to take a mortgage out on the newly renovated cottage to buy the second one and pay for the renovation. It was clear that the bank manager had no time for me. He listened to what I had to say and then told me that it was not possible to buy a property at such a low price. He then sat and looked at me for a moment, and after a slight pause, he said with a sneer

"What, have you got? .... You've got nothing!"

He then went on to tell me that he had no intention of lending me any money. So, undaunted, I went to another bank. This time in Ramsey. I was given a mortgage straight away, so I was able to set the purchase of the next property in motion. It went through very quickly and we started work repairing the derelict property across the road. By this time we had moved into the cottage that we had just completed which really was lovely. The next one had to be done on a much tighter budget so it really was a matter of just repairing it. Money was getting tight as the drinking did not slow up and there seemed to be an increasing number of hangers on. By nothing short of a miracle, we managed to get it finished. Originally the idea had been to sell the properties but by the time they were finished there was a slump in the housing market. I had gone back to doing part-time jobs, whatever I could find to bring some money in and my boyfriend was doing building work bits and pieces,whatever came his way at the time. I was to find out just what it is really like not to know what time someone is coming home and then have them come in drunk and abusive. We had been talking of getting married but now I was beginning to have grave doubts.

It occurred to me that we might try letting the houses out as self catering holiday lets for a while. It would pay the mortgage, with a bit of luck. So I worked out some advertising and had some pamphlets printed. Then I contacted local newspapers in the Dublin area and Lancashire and paid for some advertising. It was really exciting to get enquiries and we did get some bookings. But this also meant that we had to find somewhere else to live, as I had booked out both properties.

The plumber that had done the plumbing work for us owned a very delapidated house at the other side of the town and he offered us the use of it for the summer. Money was coming in now from people paying deposits for their holidays and this enabled us to put the finishing touches to the second house. I was now working part-time in an independent little grocer's nearby and also doing some cleaning work. On the day that our first guests were due to arrive in both houses, I was working in the shop and my boyfriend was doing some frantic, last minute work in the last house. I asked my boss if he would spare me for the afternoon and he said. No. I was getting frantic phone calls from my boyfriend saying he couldn't get everything done on his own in time. So I phoned my boss and told him I had to go and help and that I was sorry but I had no choice. This meant that he had to give up his Saturday afternoon and he was not amused.

So our first visitors arrived and seemed reasonably pleased with their surroundings. We went back to our hovel. We stayed there for the summer and we did manage to get quite good lettings on the cottages. Some people even booked their holidays for the following year. At the end of the season, we moved back to the second house that we had renovated, but the relationship was deteriorating. There was the responsibility of the mortgage to be met, plus I had taken out separate finance to buy furniture and bedding and all the electrical goods that were required, together with crockery, cutlery etc etc. I suppose the last straw arriving was inevitable. I was sitting in the kitchen one evening, waiting for my boyfriend to come home. Time was getting on and I knew he would have had a fair bit to drink. When he finally got back, he was drunk. I must have made some comment though I can't now remember what it was. It had an electrifying effect on him and he started shouting and bawling at me. I sat at the table looking at him and feeling quite detached. I thought, I am so tired of this abuse. I stood up and stepped towards him and slapped him hard across the face. He stopped shouting and looked as though he was going to explode with rage. I thought "Oh shit!" He lunged towards me and grabbed me by the throat. I staggered back on to the chair that I had been sitting on. He shook me about a bit and then let go. Now it was me who was angry, I stood up and stepped towards him and said

"I am not afraid of you. Now fuck off!"

He looked at me. Some sort of shock registered, and he walked very quickly away. I heard the front door slam as he left. I didn't quite know what to make of that. Three days later, he came back and asked if he could have a bath. I'd assumed that he had somewhere to stay and asked why he hadn't had a bath there. He said that he had been sleeping in his van. (This the van that I had helped him to buy, and was guarantor for.) So off he went to have a bath. In the meantime, I found every scrap of everything he owned and piled it in a heap at the bottom of the stairs. He finished his bath and came downstairs. He didn't appear to notice the mountain of his belongings at the bottom of the stairs. He headed for the kitchen.

"What are you doing?" I asked.

"Going to get a cup of tea," he replied.

But in his absence I had had what was by now becoming almost familiar, a mental shift. It wasn't good enough to come in drunk and abusive, and then disappear for three days, and then just breeze back as though nothing had happened.

"No," I said, "just fuck off, I never want to see you again.

He didn't argue, or apologise, not that it would have made any difference. I had been sickened to have been brought so low as to strike him. Even to be in that horrible situation had offended me beyond any possible reconciliation. He was a drain on my resources both financially and emotionally and I had had enough. I had promised myself after my breakdown that I would never ever let anyone put me through anything like that ever again. I was also resolved not to put up with any bad behaviour that I wouldn't have put up with from my husband. Or there would have been no point in leaving him.

Chapter 13

Douglas left school that year and was taken on at an engineering firm in Laxey where he had been on a week's work experience. No sooner had he started than he went and applied for a loan and got himself a motorbike. He was to do his City and Guilds in engineering at the local college with day release and an evening attendance. It was such a relief that he had got himself organised. He was making new friends as well and getting used to living in a different area

Things got better for me as well. One day, when I was working at a house cleaning, the manager of the local department store came to fit some curtains and we got to talking about work. He said that he had a vacancy coming up as a member of staff was retiring and he asked if I would be interested. I was. This would be my first full time job in what I thought would be a really nice place to work.

A few weeks later, I gave up the part-time work in the grocer's and also the cleaning work and started my new job. Looking after the bedding and haberdashery department in a really nice shop! The shop had three floors. On the ground floor was a lighting department, curtaining, bedding, soft furnishings, carpets and vinyls and some ornaments. The second floor was devoted to furniture and the top floor, beds. The person whose place I was taking was retiring, but she was staying on for a month so that I could get used to running my department! As it turned out, she wasn't very helpful, and didn't see why she should either advise or instruct me as she had had to pick it up herself as she went along.

The shop had a sister shop in Douglas which had a reputation for being very "posh". Both shops were owned by a national chain whose main interest was electrical goods. The shop in Ramsey adjoined to the electrical shop which had access through the furniture shop. It was such a relief have a full time job and have the company of other staff in this pleasant environment. There was a staff room where we could have a mid -morning cup of tea or coffee, and there was an hour's lunch break when I would go home and have a snack and take the dogs out. The afternoons passed just as pleasantly, with the time spent dealing with customers, checking stock and making notes of items that needed to be ordered.

The house next door to the one Douglas and I were living in had come up for sale and with my mothers help I managed to buy it. We moved in. It needed modernising but not renovating. The other two properties were now in the clear to pursue with the lettings without us constantly moving around to keep them available. But by this time, I had seriously over stretched myself financially. I had a mortgage that was being repaid over five years plus the other loans that I had taken out to furnish the cottages. I went to the bank to see if it would be possible to extend the period of the loan and so reduce the payments. The bank was not prepared to consider this and it didn't occur to me to try another bank. I just worried instead. Then one day, my friend with whom I had worked in the first pub in Castletown phoned. She had heard through someone she knew that an Indian restaurant was going to open in Ramsey and that the owners were looking for staff. She gave me a number to ring.

I rang at the weekend and enquired about evening work and was invited to go for an interview the following Wednesday afternoon which was half day closing and meant that I had the afternoon free. The people who were opening the restaurant were from Yorkshire. They spoke English with broad Yorkshire accents and they seemed very confident. I was asked if I would like to work in the bar. But a bar was the last place I wanted to work, so I said I would rather wash up. I was offered four night's work a week, Wednesday, Thursday, Friday and Saturday and would start the following week. This would mean an end to my money worries, for the time being. Since my breakdown I had continued taking sleeping tablets, so I didn't lose too much sleep over these problems. Maybe if I had, I probably wouldn't have taken so many risks. I used inhalers to control my asthma and generally I believed that I was coping.

The next Thursday duly arrived and I presented myself for the evening's washing up at the restaurant. There were only two other Indian restaurants on the Island at this time and they were both in Douglas. The people that I was working for had taken on the lease of a complex, comprising the restaurant, two bars and a disco. It was a lot to take on. They had imported bouncers from England for the disco and several members of staff. The rest was made up of local part-timers like myself. I frantically washed dishes from 7 p.m until 11.30 p.m. Any more washing up that came in after that could be left over until the next day. After four nights of this, plus the days in the shop, I was absolutely wrecked but had to carry on. In the weeks that followed I could easily fall asleep in the shop if I stood still in one place for too long. The man who was running the restaurant asked why I needed to do all the extra work and I probably gave too much information. It was a relief to talk to someone about it. He said he needed some accommodation for his staff and when he realised that my places were empty for the winter, he was keen to negotiate a price and use them. I tried to make it clear that the properties were not to be abused, as they would be used for holiday accommodation from April onwards, and that I would need his staff out, by the beginning of March. He told me not to worry and haggled with me succeeding in getting both cottages on a pretty low rent which he was going to pay weekly. So at least there was a bit more money coming in.

I still walked home from the shop at lunchtimes to let the dogs out and have my lunch. For a few weeks my estranged boyfriend would be waiting for me and wanting to patch things up. I was past patching things up and eventually he realised this and gave up. The staff from the restaurant had moved into the cottages. A couple who had met and become involved through working at the restaurant had moved into the smaller one, and the bouncers had moved into the larger one. It proved difficult, getting the weekly rental money out of the manager of the restaurant and I had to persist. The extra work proved consistent up until the New Year and then the restaurant went quiet. I ended up with one night a week washing up and the couple that were living in the small cottage were laid off. I now had to go and arrange for the social services to pay the rent. Before that though, I had had difficulty getting the rent money from their employer.

Meanwhile the chef in the restaurant was making friendly overtures to me. Of all the Indians working in the restaurant, he was the one with the poorest grasp of the English language. Despite that, he did have appeal. He was fastidiously clean and seemed very proud of his work. I tried to ignore him, but he would catch my eye while moulding the shish kebab onto a skewer and ask if I would like some of his shish kebab. I would say,

"No thank you".

But I couldn't help but smile.

A few more weeks passed and he asked if he could meet me one afternoon. I said No, that all I wanted to do was work. Nothing else. He said he was alone, and really would like to build a friendship, that it would help to pass the time. I said I was too busy and too tired to have a friend. He said he would help me. As water wears away a stone he patiently persisted. He once asked me if I would like to go to a bar for a drink and I said that I didn't drink and didn't want to spend time with people that did. So, without question, although he didn't drink much, he immediately gave up. I said that I didn't like smoking. He immediately gave that up as well. And bit by bit, I relented. If he said he would phone at a certain time, he always did. He knew that I liked walking so we took the dogs for long walks in the country. After a few weeks, I don't know why, but I asked him how old he was. He said that he was twenty six. This didn't sit too well with me as it made him nine years younger. After a few days, I told him that I was sorry but that I didn't feel happy to get involved with someone so much younger than myself. He looked very sad and then told me that, in fact, he wasn't twenty six, that he was in fact forty! This confused me no end and in the space of a minute I went from thinking that he was pretty wise for a twenty six year old to thinking that he was pretty dumb as a forty year old. Now I really couldn't cope and I said I was sorry but, No. He then said that he was in fact thirty five, which happened to be my age. Now I was annoyed and said that he had confused me and that now I would not be able to believe anything he said.

That evening, in the restaurant, he looked so sad. He told me that his heart was in his boots. He said that he would send to India for a copy of his unmarried certificate which also gave proof of his age. I didn't say anything. Not long after that, he came to see me and had with him an official unmarried certificate. But it was not his name on the certificate. I accused him of more lies. He said he had a very big problem. I asked him what it was. He told me that he had come to visit his "cousin brother" six years previously, he had come with a visa for six months, but had managed to lose his passport. Now this I could believe as he was always losing things. However, because of his poor grasp of English, he then began to find out just how difficult it was going to be for him to sort out his problem. It had begun to look impossible. He told me that he had given £400 to an Indian solicitor in Manchester but that the man had taken his money and that he had heard nothing more.

"Nobody helfing me!"he said plaintively, "All the bastad people taking my money and no helfing me."

A moments pause, "My family not helfing me, nobody helfing." "Six years," I said, "So what happened?"

He told me that his "cousin brother" told him not to worry about his passport, that he would give him work and free accommodation and pay him cash. "Easy life, no worry,forget passport." It sounded like he didn't have much choice. More problems arose when that source of work dried up and he had to find more black market employment. Within a short space of time, he was tangled up in a situation he had little hope of escaping and had eventually ended up on the Isle of Man.

I asked why he was using a different name. He said that there were only five work permits issued for the restaurant and he was using one of the names on one of the permits. He had a bank account in this name and since he lived with his employer, he used his employer's address. (Another "cousin brother"). But then he used to go to the doctor's from time to time. I asked how he managed that. He told me that "The doctors not remembering features, just seeing brown face". I thought about all the people going to the doctor, all using the same medical number and all the ailments that this one person would apparently have. It is amazing what people can get away with, but get away with it they did! If the local C.I.D turned up to check the work permits and bona fide employees, surplus workers without permits would disappear. Work permits did not have photographs of the person concerned, so the same rule applied as to the doctors. The C.I.D were always made welcome and rewarded with free meals, so I guess everybody was happy.

At heart though, I am an idealist, and my heart did go out to him with his apparently insurmountable problem. Now that I understood why he had given me the false name and lied about his age, I felt reassured. He seemed sincere and genuinely wanted to sort his problems out. He hadn't seen his parents for over six years. Our relationship was developing. I was possibly a bit broody and he was beginning to have very good husband appeal. And so, after a while, he came to stay. We still enjoyed our long walks or if he was at home, on an afternoon break from work, he would find things to do to pass the time. If there was housework to be done, he was only too happy to help. When I got back from working at the shop, I would find the house clean and the washing ironed. He would have gone to do his evening shift at the restaurant. I became very fond of him. It was not possible to say that I loved him because I didn't or maybe couldn't, perhaps I was just too worn out.

Chapter 14

March finally arrived and I was able to look forward to the winter tenants leaving. Deposits were arriving as people began to book their summer holidays. I was able to give up the night work at the restaurant. The cottages were finally vacated. The tenants from the little one were the first to find alternative accommodation. During the winter they had got themselves a puppy and a kitten. They gave the keys back to me and I went in to have my first experience of what tenants can do to a property in six months. The living room carpet was so filthy it had to be taken up and thrown out. The sofa and chairs were not just dirty, they were damaged and they had to be thrown out as well. The wall paper in the little utility room was hanging like streamers from about four feet up the wall where the puppy had been pulling it off. The little walled back garden had a thick layer of dog mess coating every inch of it. It was sickening. Fortunately, the upstairs wasn't too bad. It was cleanable and nothing was broken. I was very lucky in replacing the carpet in the living room and on the stairs. A customer of the furniture shop where I was working was replacing the carpets in a house they had bought and there was absolutely nothing wrong with the carpet that was being taken up, other than it wasn't to the new owner's taste and would have been thrown away.

The estimator for the flooring department knowing what had happened, asked if the carpet would be of any use to me. It was perfectly suitable and a huge saving as all I had to pay for was the fitting. I did have to buy new to replace the ruined furniture and this had to be paid for on one of the loan accounts I had. The little back garden had had a small lawn in the centre of it and this had been totally killed off by the stinking dog mess. We removed several inches of earth as well as the mess and replaced it with gravel.

My boyfriend was only too happy to help with sorting out the cottages. He had time on his hands during the day and liked to be kept busy. Before long we had the place clean and fresh again.

In the meantime, the tenants had moved from the larger house across the road. At that time I had 50p coin pre-payment coin meters for the electricity. The meter had been broken and the contents taken. The house inside was just dirty and only needed cleaning and decorating. My boyfriend told me not to worry that he was "helfing." He had difficulty with some of his pronunciation and "helping" came out as "helfing". He described the tenants as "dirty paky bastad people" (They were English). The spaniel 'Dusty' he called "Busty", as he couldn't manage the "D". Curiously enough,she never took to him and the first time she saw him, she growled.

If he looked at her she growled. If he took the dogs for a walk and let them off their leads, Dusty would just run straight home. Once, walking them on the other side of a stretch of water that runs from the river towards Mooragh park, he took them off their leads and Dusty took the most direct route home. She went straight to the water and swam to the other side and along the wall until she found a way up and then home. He was furious when he got back. She just snarled at him.

Still, I went to work in the shop during the week. The weekend had been spent cleaning and the house was now ready for a coat of paint. There was a large attic in this house. It had originally been divided into four small rooms. I had taken the partitions down and made it one big room. When it had been replastered I had asked for some of the stone work to be left exposed, in a random fashion, and the massive beams I just painted matt black. It was one of my favourite rooms.

My boyfriend was going to tackle the painting while I was at work. It was straight forward enough, just putting a coat of emulsion on the walls with a roller.

I had gone back to work with a lighter heart, things were getting sorted out and I was no longer in a permanent state of exhaustion. I still went home for lunch. Sometimes my boyfriend was there and sometimes he wasn't. If he wasn't busy or needed a break he would go and visit his friends or have a walk around the town. The painting on the second property was almost complete. Just the attic left to do. I was looking forward to going home that day.

The door was open on this house when I got back so I thought he must still be painting. I made my way up to the attic, feeling happy and lighthearted. The attic had a separate staircase up, with a bannister along the edge of the floor, allowing a clear view of the room. As I got far enough up the stairs to see into the room, what I saw caused my heart to sink. Every shred of happiness just evaporated and it was a while before I could speak. My boyfriend stood paintbrush in hand beaming at me.

"You like my belly beautiful stripery", he said.

My head had rapidly begun to feel like it could explode.

"You've ruined my beautiful room!"I said, aghast.

I couldn't believe the sight before me. The tenants must have been making model aircraft and he had found all the little tins of paint in a cupboard and painted not only the beams with horrible wobbly stripes but also my beautiful exposed stone wall. Each stone had been painted a different colour and the paint was running down the stones. I looked at him. Beyond speech, I turned and went home, which was next door. My head still felt like it could explode. I went to the bedroom and wrapped my head in a pillow, shutting out the world. He came up after me.

"What happened to your temperature?", he said.

He would describe a person's anger as their temperature, which is if one stops to consider it, a very accurate way of putting it.

"Berry seriously high temperature.", he observed.

I regained the power of speech.

"You've ruined my room."I said "Go away, leave me alone."

He was quiet for a moment,

"Me berry big stupid!", he said quietly. "Stupid, fucking, packy bastad, arsehole, cunt.", he said.

I just wanted him to go away.

"I'm fixing everything darling,"he said "you not too much worry, I'm fixing everything. Tomorrow I'm fixing everything," moment's pause.

"I going to work now," he said.

 I remained wrapped in my pillow.

After he had gone, I took the dogs for a walk. I couldn't go and look at the attic. The next morning he was still working at pacifying me. I was still shocked. I got up, took the dogs for a walk and then went to work. I couldn't look at him. In my mind's eye, I could still see the image of the lurid paintwork in the attic of the adjoining house. Work, mercifully, was busy and the morning passed quickly. I went home for lunch and took the dogs out. I didn't go next door. I did not know what I would find next and I had no idea how he was going to rectify the mess.

After a few days, he told me that he had "fixed" the painting and I ventured to have a look. The beams were painted black again. He had painted the random, exposed stones white. There wasn't any other option really, it must have taken many layers of paint. And so once again, his seemingly genuine desire to work at our friendship won me over and we were friends again.

Chapter 15

Bookings and deposits were coming in steadily now for the cottages and by the end of April they were booked for the season. My outgoings were still quite high but this second season was bringing in more money and it was beginning to look like I could settle into some sort of routine.

But, alas, changes were in the offing. The company that owned the furniture shop where I worked, had their main interest in electrical retail, and had decided that they no longer wanted to be involved with the furniture retail. However, in order to save jobs in the shop where I worked three members of staff decided to raise the necessary finance to take over the business. Namely, the manager, the accountant and the flooring fitter. They were enthusiastic and thought that they could really turn things around. Everything was going to be better. Sadly, it did not work out. Changes were made, the working environment was no longer quite so carefree and happy. The self esteem and confidence of the staff was affected. People began to leave. The manager, once happy and approachable, became bad tempered and moody.

The lady who ran the curtain department, who had become my friend, walked out one day after a row. She didn't come back but went immediately to work for a rival firm. The day that she walked out was, by coincidence, the day that I had planned to give a month's notice. After the row, the manager, clearly shaken, came and asked what I thought and I told him that it had been my intention to give them a month's notice on that day.

"Oh" he said, "you'd better go and tell the accountant."

So I did, and that was that.

I had decided that I would make a living working from

home, making curtains and blinds. When I had married Douglas's father, I became a housewife and stayed at home to look after Douglas. I had made all our clothes. I had also made curtains, blinds and quite a lot of soft furnishings. I had been studying 'O' level needlework at school but did not take the exam since my mother's second marriage had ended halfway through my 'O' level studies and the next school that I went to did not include needlework as an 'O' level subject. However I had learnt enough about tailoring for it to be useful to me. I had picked up extra tips about curtain making at the furniture store and had, on occasion, made curtains for them when they had had orders that were required urgently. I was reasonably confident that I could make a living. I worked my month's notice.

Meanwhile Douglas was still working for the engineering firm in Laxey but he was lax about attending college for his City and Guilds qualification. Despite that, he was managing to pass his exams. So I didn't worry too much. On the whole, he was no trouble and I loved having him at home. Every stage of his life was fascinating. He wasn't an angel, but then who is? I couldn't claim to be an angel either but usually I did try to do the right thing.

There seemed to be a big demand for people working from home, making curtains and blinds and I had no trouble reeling the work in. There was a very large first floor bedroom in the cottage. It had been two rooms and the previous owner had knocked the two into one. I managed to obtain a large table to work on,the folding type that is used on market stalls and I set this up at one end of the bedroom. I could literally get out of bed, put on a tracksuit and walk across the room to work.

The people that I began to do the curtain work for would turn up with rolls of curtain material and lining fabric and boxes of various types of heading tape and neatly printed out, the required dimensions. I would take these upstairs and stack them in my room. I began to feel a bit like the "miller's daughter" in the fairy story who had to spin straw into gold, except that no goblin turned up secretly at night to do it for me. My boyfriend was, as usual, still supportive and would patiently press the finished work for me. It was, though, the loneliest job that I had ever done. As the months passed, I was finding it increasingly difficult to get motivated and I knew that I would have to make a change.

I began looking in the paper for something else to do. I noticed that the Government offices were advertising for temporary staff to work for a minimum of six months, transferring all the company file details onto computer. I thought I might have enough typing skills to do that and so I applied and got an "interview". The interview was straight forward enough, all I had to do was copy type a sheet of A4 print. I managed that and got my six months work. My bank manager was delighted. He had a vision of me settling into permanent employment at the Government offices.

I didn't fall in love with my job at the Government offices. The office that I worked in was below ground level and had no windows. There was noisy, antiquated air conditioning. The ceiling was painted black and the strip lights had special covers on which were supposed to diffuse the harsh lighting. To cope with this, I had to be out with the dogs by six in the morning and give them a good long walk before leaving them shut in for the day. I then caught a bus into Douglas. This situation was relieved somewhat by a neighbour who worked in the same office and offered me lifts to and from work. There was something quite surreal about working in this office. The people that worked there seemed to be half mad with the routine and the lack of stimulation and would play pranks on each other, hurl insults and just behave as if they were barking …mad. The gentle folks that I had met in the mental hospital seemed totally sane by comparison. They were there because life had got a too much for them, whereas these people did seem to be completely, permanently, round the twist.

The six months was almost over. The office supervisor asked me what typing certificates I had, and, seemed quite put out to learn that I had none and was largely self taught. On top of that, apart from art, I had no 'O' level passes, so I didn't need to be a genius to work out that there would be no long term future for me here. "O" level passes are required if one wants to succeed in office work.

It was time to start worrying about my next source of income. I started looking in the Situations Vacant column in the local papers. Then I found it! Something completely different. A market garden in the North of the Island was advertising for staff to work in the greenhouses. Sounded like heaven to me. I rang up and spoke to the manager and arranged to go and meet him. I had to catch a bus to get there and to my relief, was given the job. I would start a week later. One of my friends reassured me that people who worked with plants were usually really nice and down to earth. Things were looking up again, but,I didn't have a car and I would need one to get to work on time. I began looking through the ads in the paper and noticed a Fiat 600 for sale for £75, I rang up, and enquired about it and was told that it was not possible to drive the car because the gasket on the water pump had gone. I phoned my brother and told him about it. He told me to take a selection of spanners and a piece of cereal packet and some gasket gum and told me to offer £50 for the car. If the offer was accepted, I was to give the man selling it cash and then do a quick repair on the car. He explained how to make a gasket out of the cereal packet and how to replace the one on the water pump.

I phoned back the owner of the car and arranged to go and see it the next day. Meanwhile I borrowed some spanners from a neighbour and bought some gasket gum and got my piece of cereal packet ready. The next afternoon I set off for Laxey where the car was for sale. I found the house and in the drive was a very forlorn looking little car. It had been hand painted in a shade of turquoise blue and had a long strip of foam stuck down the hinged edge of the drivers door, also painted turquoise blue. The car's owner explained that the driver's door had been caught in a gale force wind and that he now used the passenger door to get in and out. He climbed in and started the engine to prove that it would start.

I asked if he would take £50 for it and he said he would, so I handed over the £50 cash that I had taken with me. I then asked if he would mind if I made a temporary gasket for the water pump. He watched me curiously, while I followed my brother's instructions. I was surprised how easy it was. I then topped up the water in the radiator and thanked the, by now, astonished former owner of the car.

"If I'd known that was all there was to it," he said, "I would have done it myself and charged a hundred and fifty pounds."

I shrugged my shoulders and smiled and climbed into my new car, started it and drove off triumphantly. The former owner had warned me that the brakes weren't too good and that I might need to pump them a bit. I bore this in mind and drove home slowly and carefully.

Chapter 16

The weekend passed without further incident or excitement. My son and his friends thought my new car a huge joke and did not want to be seen near it and certainly not in it. Guests arrived and were settled into the cottages. I walked the dogs and anticipated happier times. My boyfriend was intrigued with the car and that I had managed the small repair.

We had settled into quite a comfortable routine now. He still helped with what he could. At the weekends we went for long walks with the dogs and then came back to beautifully cooked meals. I was quite happy again.

Monday morning arrived, and I set off for work. The market garden was about six miles away, down very quiet country roads, so I didn't worry too much about my car. What a change from going into Douglas to work in an office. I arrived just before 8 'o' clock and went, as instructed, to the packing shed. The manager was there and the supervisor who I hadn't met. A lady who lived next door and worked part-time had arrived just before me and the sound of car tyres crunching on the gravel drive announced someone else arriving. A car door was heard to open and then shut, and then there was the sound of footsteps. A young woman breezed in, she was introduced and started up a lively and cheeky banter with her boss. Two men arrived next, within minutes of each other, one of retirement age and one in his early twenties. So, seven staff, quite a lot, really, I thought. With the exception of the youngest of the two men and myself, everyone else was part-time, apart from the manager and the supervisor.

Work began in the packing shed, with the tomatoes and cucumbers picked the previous day being packed. Tomatoes were graded by colour and cucumbers by length. Everyone was involved and the chatter was non-stop as the work progressed. What a change from the government offices. The packing out of the way, it was time for a tea break before the next part of the days routine. After the break, it was time to move on to the picking. The lady who lived in the next door property went off to pick flowers which were grown in polytunnels. The manager came into the greenhouse to explain to me how the tomatoes should be picked. Roughly half the greenhouse was given over to tomatoes planted in the earth and the other half was given over to tomatoes grown hydroponically..

Crates on wheeled trollies were pushed down the rows of tomatoes. We picked only a certain band of colour ripeness, picking down one side of the row, going up and the other side, going back. Each aisle produced around four crates of tomatoes and the whole greenhouse had to be picked. This took us up to lunchtime. The young woman, and the young man and myself picked tomatoes. When the tomato picking was finished, the young woman went home. The older man looked after the cucumber house. He was usually finished by lunchtime and would then go home.

That left me and the young man. We ate our sandwiches in the sunshine outside the greenhouse. He brought a radio with him and loved the sixties music. He had a collection of tapes with all his favourites on, my favourites too, so the day had got off to a good start.

Lunch over, the next task was trimming the tomatoes. Side shoots had to be taken out and the leaves cut away from the ripening trusses. The new growth at the top of the plants was carefully wound around strings tied to rods that ran the width of the greenhouse. We worked through the plants, starting at one end, row by row. It took several days to deal with the whole greenhouse. All the while there was the accompaniment of the Stones, Beatles, Beachboys, Donovan and Bob Dylan, to name but a few. Work would finish at four in the afternoon. So the first couple of days were pretty lighthearted.

The young woman never stopped talking. When the tomato sorting was finished, she carried on the banter in the greenhouse. Initially it was directed at the young man. All manner of salacious innuendo and sarcasm. I knew I would have difficulty coping if she started on me. A few days passed and she started asking questions about my home life. I don't like being grilled about my home life by nosey strangers, and giving evasive answers, without actually offending, soon began to be a problem. Things got complicated when she wanted to come and visit me and I said that I was sorry but I really hadn't got the time. It was true, I hadn't got the time but I didn't want her hanging around. She took this as a rejection, which indeed it was, though I had intended it to be a gentle rejection.

After that the whole atmosphere changed. She was pleasant enough in the packing shed, but as soon as we got into the greenhouse she would start, going on and on about my work, criticizing and finding fault as she tore tomatoes off the plants in an effort to pick more than me. I managed to put up with this for a couple of months, but one day I snapped. I started off by asking her if she had nothing better to do than criticize what I was doing, and suggested that she take a look at what she was doing, which was pretty rough. Once I started, I couldn't stop and she fled, in tears, to the supervisor.

Very soon, the supervisor arrived with the tearful woman, not looking at all pleased with me. The story went that I had laid into the young woman, verbally, and given her hell. Which was true enough, I had. But as I explained, she had been picking on me for weeks, criticizing and finding fault, and I just got sick of it. I said. Not to worry, that I would leave. The supervisor then wanted to go and get the manager. So the manager arrived, and again I offered to leave. He persuaded me to stay and said that he would separate us. And so I went to work in the cucumber house. The old man was about to retire, so it did fit in.

Unfortunately, my self-esteem had dropped to a low level, which wasn't helped by the fact that my persecutor chose to carry on and would come across to the cucumber house when she knew that she could do it unnoticed and carry on as before. While all this was going on, my Indian boyfriend had begun to have problems of his own. There were problems at the restaurant, and trade had begun to fall off and eventually my boyfriend was laid off. A friend of his, in Scotland, offered him black market work. He did try staying but couldn't cope with having nothing to do and no money coming in. One of the things I did always like about him was that (apart from the disastrous paint job in the house next door), he did find ways to pass the time. He would get my sewing machine out and make things (usually bags) from scraps of material.

He did the football pools, and would have a bath and put clean clothes on and his turban and then ask his Indian God, whose picture hung on the bedroom wall, to let him win the Pools. This didn't happen, and so arrangements were made and soon after, he left for Scotland, where he had been based before he came over to the Isle of Man.

Chapter 17

I was once again back to assessing my financial situation, having tried unsuccessfully to get the bank to extend the period over which my mortgage was being paid and so reduce the payments. I only had about four weeks left of holiday payments to come in, then that source of income stopped. It looked like the Indian restaurant was heading for bankruptcy. There was prospect of more dodgy winter tenants and the cost of putting right the damage they did. However it was a bit late in the day to make any changes, so I carried on. Some of my neighbours had decided that they wanted a change and had put their house up for sale. They wanted a property to renovate. Things happened quite quickly for them. They found a property nearby that they liked and managed to find a buyer for their property, all within the space of a few weeks. Since the property that they were going to buy needed quite a lot of work doing to it, they asked if they could rent one of the cottages for the winter. So that was a start. All I had to do was find short term tenants for the other property.

Once again, fortune favoured me. A company based in Manchester specialising in weather proof exterior coatings, had painters working on the Island and they needed temporary accommodation and out of the blue, got in touch with me. This from my advert in the Tourist Board guide. I told them that I needed he property vacated by the beginning of March and this was acceptable and so it looked like I would manage to limp financially through another winter.

My boyfriend came back for a visit a few weeks later and we talked about sorting out his problems, getting married and starting up our own place over here. I liked the idea. In fact, I loved the idea.

Meanwhile the harassment at the Nurseries continued and my self-esteem got so low I was losing the will to work. I went to see the manager and told him what was happening and that I was sorry, but I couldn't cope and would have to leave. He was sympathetic and suggested that rather than me just leave, he would lay me off and that way I would be able to claim the dole. I was grateful, I had never been on the dole and was curious to see what it would be like. I signed on, and a week later went to collect my money. I lasted three months, it was awful, there was something about the whole experience that I found both degrading and humiliating.

I had always liked the idea of working in a ladies dress shop and saw in the paper a vacancy advertised in Douglas. I thought how nice it would be to work selling lovely clothes and so I applied. But, alas, I was not successful. Then I noticed a position in a shop in Ramsey on an industrial estate that sold pictures and mirrors among other things, basic office skills were needed so I applied for that. I had to take an IQ test and I didn't get that either. They were kind enough to tell me that I had been pipped at the post by a former bank manager. There was at least some consolation in that.

Looking through the situations vacant in the local papers I saw an advert for an assistant in another dress shop, this time in Ramsey. I wrote and applied for that but was unlucky again. Then I saw an advert requiring an assistant in a Gents' Outfitters, also in Ramsey, I applied for that and this time I was lucky. The shop was run by a woman who had worked there for over fifty years. She was over 70. Another woman came in and just worked mornings. It really wasn't that bad. The woman that came in in the mornings was a delight to work with, though the manageress could be a bit cold. It was interesting nonetheless. I learned how to measure and was soon able to advise on what size a man would need for suits, shirts, jackets etc and because of all my sewing experience, I did occasional alterations as well. Financially life was easier, but this lateral course was now waiting to be followed. If I was to be able to help to resolve my husband's immigration problems and pursue our dream of having our own business, I would need to release some funds and the only way it seemed that I could do that would be by selling one of the cottages. However I had already taken some holiday bookings for the next summer, so plans would have to be put on hold for a while.

Chapter 18

Meanwhile the exterior coating company that had got in touch with me over the winter let for their employees had installed two young men in the larger of the two properties that I used for the lettings. They had been in a few weeks when one of them came to see me and said that he hadn't been married very long and very much missed his wife and their baby. Since it was quite a large house he wanted to know if it would be alright if his wife and baby came over. I wasn't keen, but he said that she would be able to look after the place. Eventually I relented. Then he asked if it would be alright if she brought their puppy as well. I explained about all the damage and mess I had had to deal with the last time tenants had brought animals into one of the houses, and he assured me that his wife would see to it that the house was kept in good order and that the puppy wouldn't do any damage. I relented, and a week later his pretty, petite, peroxide blond wife arrived with the baby and puppy, which happened to be a Rotweiller. I began to have misgivings but hoped for the best.

Some time later her husband called to say that the television wasn't working. I said I would sort it out for them, and decided to go through the back yard gate to the back door. I had to struggle to get the yard gate open, the reason for which soon became apparent, as I pushed and shoved at the stubborn gate. There was a strata of giant dog shit which was rising like a wave behind the gate as I pushed. Having got the gate open, enough to squeeze through, I had to navigate the gaps in between the piles of poo to get to the back door. I knocked.

The wifey came to the door, cigarette in hand and led me into the sitting room. On the way through I noticed the panel doors gouged and scratched by the dog and that generally the place was mucky and beginning to have a heavy smell. I checked the television while worrying about what to do about the tenants. Leaving by the front door, I decided I had no choice but to ring the exterior coating company and get them to move their staff, because if I let them stay, the house was going to be in a bad state in a short space of time.

The company were very good about the problem that their staff were causing me and they were moved out very quickly. I decided to leave the house empty for the rest of the winter and take my time getting it ready for the summer lettings. The people in the smaller cottage had got their next property in reasonable order and they had moved into it. It was time to re-decorate again. I suppose that if money had been the be-all and end-all in my life I would not have had a problem with the annual big clean and redecorate that was the routine for the cottages. Maybe if I had been able to negotiate a better mortgage deal with lower payments spread over a longer term, I might have managed a different perspective. The mortgage only had five years to run and stood at roughly £5000 which twenty years on, seems so little. At the time though, I was finding the payments crippling.

About a week after the weather coating people moved out of the larger house I went in to assess how much I had to do, clearing the yard of dog mess, then just cleaning and repainting. There was a lot of cleaning to do. The grill pan was almost full to the brim with rancid fat, a fire just waiting to happen. At the time I felt disgusted that people could be so careless and live with such a risk. Many years later, it would occur to me that it was possible that they really couldn't help the way they were and just didn't have the mental capacity to see the dangers.

Chapter 19

I had been working at the Gents' Outfitters for four months. When I wasn't actually selling clothes or unpacking and pricing new stock, the stock on hangers needed to be constantly re-hung, put in order, kept free of dust. Sitting down was not an option. Mirrors were strategically placed around the shop so that the manageress from her glass fronted cubical/office could keep a watchful eye on all things at all times. Unbeknown to her, I was working on my escape.

The summer was passing. My boyfriend came for short visits when he could. We were both committed to resolving all the problems and starting our own small business here. Once again, I felt sure that a better life was both possible and waiting for me, for us. I had decided that I would put the smallest of the cottages up for sale at the end of the season. Meanwhile, my boyfriend was trying to find a reliable Indian solicitor to sort out his immigration problems.

During the summer I had taken one booking for the following year from some people who had stayed in the smallest of the cottages and wanted to make sure of their reservation for the following year. I hadn't taken a deposit saying that we could sort that out nearer the time. It came as a great relief to put the first property up for sale and not to have the worry of finding tenants for the short winter lets. I contacted the people who had made a provisional booking for the following summer and made my apologies to them as I would not be continuing with the holiday lettings. The husband was angry and ranted for a while before accepting that he would need to find alternative accommodation.

Fortunately the cottage sold quickly, within weeks, and I was able to pay off the mortgage and buy myself a reasonable second hand car. When my boyfriend came to visit, we started looking for a property that we could turn into a takeaway or small restaurant. There didn't seem to be much on the market at that time, and as we were both filled with an almost overwhelming impatience to make changes, this was to be a frustrating time.

Soon though, I had a phone call from my boyfriend to say that he had found a good solicitor. The man in question was a Sikh and had had a university education and also was the chief Immigration Officer for Middlesex. I felt secure in the knowledge that this was the man who could be relied on to sort out all the immigration problems.

An appointment was made to visit him and discuss our problems and work to resolve them. My boyfriend came over for a break and I booked the car on the ferry. He told me that I had to bring £2000 in cash for the solicitor. I thought that this was a bit odd but went along with it. The day before we left, I drew £2000 from the bank. The next day, we went on the morning ferry to Liverpool. From there, I drove to Wiltshire and we spent the next night with my family there. The next day I drove to Middlesex where we had an appointment to meet Professor B. our solicitor, at 1 p.m. I managed to find his home, which also served as his office, without too much difficulty. It was a rather palatial bungalow with two entrances, a sweeping driveway and plenty of room for parking.

I was feeling nervous, but felt there was no turning back. It had occurred to me, more than once, that maybe somewhere along the line, I hadn't worked hard enough at my first marriage. I had resolved to do my absolute best at the second one that I was inevitably going to have.

We rang the door bell and waited. The door was answered by an Indian woman who introduced herself as the Professor's wife and explained that she also worked as his secretary.

We were ushered into an enormous sitting room that housed many chairs and several sofa's. We sat down and waited. Mrs B. brought us tea and biscuits. The room suggested that these were wealthy and influential people. There was a photograph of Professor B. with Margaret Thatcher and other M.P's at that time.

My initial nervousness began to abate. Everything would work out. Eventually Mrs B. reappeared and we were taken to a small office and introduced to Professor B. A tall heavy man with his long beard in a neat roll net. He wore a black turban and looked most impressive, most professional. He asked my boyfriend questions in Punjabi before turning his attention to me. It didn't occur to me to doubt his sincerity. I confirmed my boyfriend's story. At least, I think I did. In hindsight, they could have been discussing the weather for all I knew. I also confirmed that I had the £2000 in cash with me. I felt uneasy about handing it over. But then,considering Professor B's high profile, I didn't think he would do anything dishonest.

Next he brought out some magazines, he showed me pictures of men who had been killed. He told me that Sikhs were being persecuted and killed and that if my boyfriend were to be deported this was the fate that was waiting for him. Predictably I was horrified. Having listened to our story, Professor B. then explained that he would be able to open a case and act for us. He would write a letter of introduction and explanation which we would then have to take to the Home Office at Croyden to register the case. He also wrote a letter of introduction to the M.P. Who represented the area where my boyfriend was living (and working on the black market) at the time, in Coatbridge in Scotland. We were to go first to the Home Office and register my boyfriend's application for political asylum. We were then to go to Scotland and meet the M.P. Who, upon reading Professor B's letter would confirm our relationship and also give us a letter of introduction to give to the local Registrar who would be conducting our marriage.

Chapter 21

Leaving Middlesex, we drove to Croyden and found a hotel near to the Home Office. Professor B. had advised us to be at the Home office as early as possible and had suggested no later than 8 a.m. Things were running comparatively smoothly. The next day, we left our hotel around 7.30 a.m. By the time we had parked and walked to the offices it was just after 8 a.m.

An amazing sight greeted us, a long queue had already formed, made up of many different nationalities, some people were in national dress. The day began to feel unreal. We joined the queue and waited. By 9 a.m it was very long and winding and was taking on a carnival appearance.

There was movement at the front. The Office had opened and we began to slowly move forward. When we got to the door, we were given a ticket with a number on it and directed to a large waiting room. This room had row upon row of benches facing an equally long counter with many windows in it. Behind each window sat a clerk. Above each window was a box with numbers on it. We sat and waited for the number on our ticket to come up on one of the boxes. A couple of hours later, it did. The procedure was very straight forward. We simply registered the application by handing over Professor B's letter. That was it. Time to go and get something to eat and head off to Scotland for the next stage of our mission. Things were shaping up nicely. What was I worried about?

It is a long drive to Scotland from Croyden and by the time we got to the Lake District I was tired and would like to have stopped for the night and carried on the next day. My boyfriend, however, was anxious to press on and so, after a short rest, we carried on. We spent the night with some people he knew in Glasgow. The next day we had to meet the M.P. Professor B. had already spoken to him so he would be expecting us. I just had to ring and make an appointment to see him. We met him in the afternoon and went over our story again and gave him Professor B.'s letter of introduction. So much help and support was given. Next, we went to meet the Registrar and set a date for our wedding!

We were going to get married on the 17th of August 1989.

That was all that could be done for the time being. We spent one more night with my boyfriend's friends. I had taken a few days holiday leave that was due to me and was going home the next day, leaving early in the morning to catch the afternoon boat. I was feeling better, my boyfriend's immigration problems were receding by the day. Soon they would just be a memory.

It was summertime, August was approaching and so was August 17th. My son Douglas was going to come up to Scotland with me and actually give me away. On the 16th of August we caught the morning boat to Heysham and set off for Coatbridge. When we were on the M8 I was suddenly seized with overwhelming doubts. I said to my son.

"I don't feel right about this anymore, I feel like I want to turn round and go home."

My son suggested that it was just pre-wedding nerves and that I would be alright when we got there. So I kept going, I had phoned my boyfriend to say what time I thought we would arrive. He had booked us into a hotel in Coatbridge and was waiting on the roadside when we arrived. He looked lost and anxious and pleased to see us and I felt guilty about how I had felt on the motorway. We parked in the hotel carpark and went to check in. It looked quite grand on the outside. Inside was a bit disappointing. The rooms were even more disappointing, grubby, and the bedding looked like it hadn't been changed. My son said that his room was in a similar state. So we checked out and found another hotel.

The day wore on. We were all tired and decided to have a meal at the hotel and have an early night. The restaurant was busy and we waited ages for our food. We were then kept awake most of the night by the noisy hotel Disco.

However, the morning of the 17th duly arrived. I wanted to go into the town and buy a corsage for myself and carnations for my boyfriend and son to wear. My boyfriend came with me and seemed unusually bad tempered. However his mood improved after we had been back to the hotel and got changed and set off for the Registry. His mood improved still further when he was greeted by some of his friends that were going to attend the wedding. He had asked if he could have the wedding vows translated to him in Punjabi by one of his friends.

We went in and were greeted by the Registrar, a very warm motherly looking woman who made us feel very welcome. There we were in the Registry, taking our vows, my boyfriend having the vows translated to him in Punjabi which seemed to be causing him great amusement and to which he enthusiastically responded with many "Oh, yes'es,"

His friends thought the proceedings hilarious too. Even the Registrar was affected by all the jollity and was having difficulty not joining in. It was the most cheerful wedding I had ever been to.

The formalities over, we signed the Register,and took some photographs. We were now Mr and Mrs Ram. We went for a celebration drink in a nearby bar. I asked what was so funny at the Registry. The truth was that the vows hadn't been translated at all, instead his friend had made suggestions about what was going to happen later on that evening. After spending some time in the bar we went back to the place where my husband's friends worked and had a meal, before setting off to spend the rest of the evening in a nightclub in Glasgow's docklands. All in all, it hadn't been such a bad day. The next day Douglas was going to go back to the Island by plane and I and my now husband were going to pay a brief visit to his brother in Nottingham.

By the time we got to Nottingham I was very aware of a change coming over my husband. Even his facial features seemed changed. I would say that there was malice in his expression. It worried me, but I consoled myself with the thought that when we managed to sort out the work issue and he had a new sense of purpose, everything would be alright.

Chapter 22

We had to go back and see professor B. now that we were married. He took a copy of our wedding certificate and sent an accompanying letter to the Home Office. He spoke to my husband at length in Punjabi and told me that he had told my husband that he was fortunate and that he should look after me. I wasn't altogether sure that I believed him. He then told me that it would help my husband's case if I were to have a baby. For years I had longed for a cosy family environment. But my reply did not reflect this. Instead I said I could not have a baby in order to further my husbands appeal for asylum. To me it would be using a child as a pawn and I wasn't prepared to do that. Besides this was potentially was another niggling parallel to my mothers life. She had two sons with her second husband before the marriage ground to an end, and I certainly did not want to end up in a similar predicament.

Besides my unspoken doubts. I had a new husband with whom I was not feeling particularly cosy at the moment.

We had now done all we could for the time being. I took my husband back to Scotland and then I went back to the Isle of Man and my job at the Gents' Outfitters.

Every crisis I had weathered brought with it a new and useful skill, no matter how small. I learnt how to shorten jacket sleeves and how to take in or let out waistbands on trousers. This, on top of the knowledge of measuring that I was acquiring. Working in the shop did rather cause me to see the customers (the men and their wives, the ones who thought they were irresistible, the ones that wished to draw attention to their wealth, the married ones who liked to flirt), in a different perspective.

Men would come into the shop and, ask, suggestively, if I would like to measure their inside leg. I would dispatch them to a changing cubicle and ask them to remove their trousers, saying I would measure the inside leg that way. If the manageress was in the shop, she would have no hesitation doing this measurement and would give the tape measure a good push in the crotch area. I never heard her actually ask which side a man dressed. Sometimes a normally timid married man would venture into the shop without his wife and buy something for himself. Invariably, he would be brought back soon after, with his wife and the offending purchase. He would stand meekly by, whilst his wife spoke about him as a third party and asked for the offending item to be exchanged.

All sorts of people came for all sorts of things. It was an old fashioned shop, selling traditional menswear and I did like that aspect of it. But not enough to stay for ever. I was considering putting the second property up for sale rather than leave it empty for the winter. However, fate intervened again and some people I was acquainted with got in touch. They had heard through a friend that I had a house empty and asked if they could use it for a while. Having sold a property, they had been abroad for a long break and were now renting a place while they looked for somewhere else to buy. They had some problem with the property, that they were renting, and had decided to look for another temporary place, which is how they came to contact me. I didn't see any reason why not, I would have no worries about the place being abused as they were clean and tidy people. However, a new and different problem arrived with them. The husband had not met my Indian husband and when he did, he berated me about the situation that I was getting myself into. His criticism was vicious, offensive and relentless. He said my husband had seen me as a wealthy woman and would just be using me to his own ends. I was appalled by this and hoped they would not stay too long.

My marriage, as it happened, was not unpleasant, in fact, if anything, it was happier than theirs. My husband did not treat me like a servant, was not rude to my friends, and continued to visit when he could. Our search for premises continued. We had noticed a large empty commercial building towards the end of the main shopping street. It had been an outlet for cut price furniture but was now empty and a hand written FOR SALE sign was stuck on the window. We had passed this place several times without it catching our interest but, today the door was open and so we went in.

It happened to be the owner, and his business partner who were inside, and we asked if it would be possible to have a look round. The place was semi-derelict and comprised of three properties. Two had made up the furniture store and the third was rented by a chain of newsagents. The back yard was a ramshackle assortment of decaying sheds.

There were two floors above the shops which were in reasonable order. The asking price was £84,000 It seemed a reasonable price for the property and I had no difficulty in seeing the potential. Moreover, I was not put off by the thought of the work that had to be done. This property would present a huge challenge. My husband liked it too. And so I said I would go and have a chat with the bank manager.

Chapter 23

Whilst the bank manager did not dismiss my plan, he was very cautious. I had asked about the possibility of having a mortgage to buy the property,in order that I could use the proceeds from the sale of the cottages for the necessary renovation work and setting up of the restaurant. He said that in order for this to be considered,I would need to do cash forecasts to show that the estimated income would be sufficient to cover mortgage payments,overheads wages, etc.

When things fall easily into place, it is also all too easy to believe that a situation is meant to be. And so when things began to fall into place I found the confidence to continue down, what was to be, my road to Hell. I needed to find an accountant to help me with the cash forecasts. The self-employed husband of one of my friends was friendly with an accountant who dealt with his accounts. The accountant had mentioned that he quite liked the idea of doing the accounts for a restaurant. He seemed intrigued with helping me to provide 3 years cashflow forecasts for the bank. We spent hours working out the minimum turnover that could be expected that would still cover the necessary overheads. Armed with this, about a month later, we both attended the bank for a meeting with the manager. He picked through our carefully worked out figures and asked questions here and there. My now accountant dealt with the questions,giving appropriate and valid answers. Finally the manager looked up, pushed the papers away and said,

"I can't help you with this."

It was a rhetorical statement. No reply was needed. All that was required was for us to leave. However, in the few seconds it took for the manager to make the statement and for me to take it in, the scenario suddenly began to feel ridiculous and I began to laugh. The accountant seemed most embarrassed by this and we quickly left the office. We went back to his office, a few streets away and he asked me what I had found so funny. It was the manager's huge sense of power that had amused me. I had the impression that he scoffed at the cashflow figures that we had produced and had enjoyed pushing them away with a flourish. I apologised if I had embarrassed him with my reaction.

It was agreed that I would approach other banks. But on my own now, as I knew roughly how the interview would go. I was not successful with any of the other banks that I tried which did not surprise me since I was not a known customer to them. I took stock of the situation and came to terms with the fact that this project was not going to be possible after all. With regret, I phoned my husband and told him that I could not manage to arrange a mortgage and so we would have to keep looking. I got in touch with the owner of the property and told him that I had not been able to arrange a mortgage and so had no further interest in the purchase of the property. Meanwhile,though, he was having no luck in finding a buyer.

A few days later, he came to the door of the shop and handed me a note, written on an address page, torn from a diary.

"JUNE PLEASE RING ME AFTER 5. I THINK I CAN HELP YOU"

I rang when I got home. He said that after a lot of consideration,he was prepared to offer me a private mortgage. We talked on. He said the offer would be the full amount based on the full asking price of the property at a rate of 16%, re-payable over a period of 18 years. Mortgage rates were around 14% at that time and it was usual for a private mortgage to be set at a higher rate. I still wasn't daunted and rang my husband to explain to him this new development. We decided to go ahead. But before anything official was signed, I told my potential mortgagee that I would need to apply for permission for change of use on the property.

Once again, things began to run smoothly and once again, things began to fall into place. I was aware of the risk that I was taking, but felt that in view of the fact that the property was semi-derelict and was about to have £140K + invested into it, that even if the worst came to the worst, I should at least be able to break even and be able to cut my losses and come out with enough to buy a small property.

Events progressed. The application for change of use appeared in the paper. When I arrived at work the day after the paper came out, the manageress came out of her cubicle holding the local paper, slammed it down on the counter, and demanded to know what was going on. She was furious at the prospect of me leaving, which in turn made me most anxious to leave.

Subsequently the change of use was approved and the purchase of the property went ahead and was completed at the end of June 1990. I went to see my bank manager and told him of the developments. He put his head in his hands and said.

"Oh, no, What have you done!"

To which I replied that I felt that there just had to be more to life than the life I was living.

My solicitor advised caution when it came to putting my husband's name on the deeds to the property as joint owner. I did not believe that my husband would deceive me and he became joint owner of the property. The weeks were slipping by. I decided to hand in my notice at the Gents' Outfitters, in order to give this new project my full attention. Meanwhile the couple who were renting from me found somewhere else to stay temporarily, where they could take their furniture, so they moved out and I was glad to see them go. The property could now be put up for sale.

My husband seemed happy to leave everything up to me. He was living in Scotland until I sorted out our new life. He had no worries and no responsibilities. I left the Gents' Outfitters at the end of September 1990. I now had to enlist the services of an architect to draw up plans for turning the building into a restaurant.

Many things had to be taken into consideration, besides the structural work. The restaurant area had to be planned and the kitchen area. The amount of seating, and based on that, the number of toilets, male and female to be provided. New mains would have to be installed. For me, it was a big project. However, the plans were duly completed and passed. The mortgage was being paid from the proceeds of the sale from the first cottage.

The eldest of my two brothers had been doing building work in the area where they lived in Wiltshire and was enthusiastic about coming to work on the project. Because of my previous experience with building firms, I had decided from the start that I would manage the project. Things still running smoothly, the plans were passed and the second property also sold reasonably quickly.

A work permit was obtained for my brother. Douglas also came to work with us and on December 1st 1990 we began to work on demolishing the assortment of rickety buildings at the back of the property. Skip after skip was filled with rubble.

On the 12th of December I received a letter from H..M. IMMIGRATION OFFICE at Glasgow Airport. Professor B. Had told us that we would be interviewed by immigration officials at some point, to assess whether our marriage was genuine and not just a marriage of convenience to enable my husband to stay in the country. The interview was to take place on the 11th of January 1991 at 11 a.m. My husband came over for a few days at Christmas and we went over and over his story, as it had happened, how we met, where etc etc. Professor B. had assured us that there was nothing to worry about as the Authorities were prepared to consider the cases of people who came forward voluntarily.

Meanwhile,many more skips were filled with rubble and by the end of the month, the demolition was completed. My husband came over, as before,and helped when he could. He was irritable though and managed to cause friction whenever he was around. It was decided that I would fly to Glasgow on the early flight on the 11th of January for the interview with the Immigration Authorities. My husband would meet me off the plane and we would sit in the airport cafe and go over our details together. I reassured my husband that there was absolutely nothing to worry about as we had been open and honest at all times.

Eleven o'clock came round and we made our way to the Immigration Office. We were interviewed separately by different officers and asked a variety of questions to which our answers should be the same. The interviews only lasted about 10 minutes and it was a relief to have them over with. Soon after this, my husband's application was accepted. A passport was issued to him. He was given a National Health number and a National Insurance number. His stay in the country was now legal. All we had to now was get him additional permission to work on the Island.

Chapter 24

My brother seemed happy enough and perfectly capable of working to the plans. Through the winter, work progressed. Footings were dug and the new extension at the back of the building which was to form the restaurant kitchen, store room and extra dining room area quickly took shape. Ambitiously, I had hoped work could be completed by April, but we sailed past that deadline and the next one. I put the last property up for sale and my brother decided that he would like to buy it so that was a very easy sale. Finally, it looked like we should be able to aim for opening in August. Money was getting swallowed up very quickly now and more had to be raised. My husband managed to borrow money from members of his family, which, to me, confirmed his commitment to the project. Indeed, I thought it only right that he should make a contribution.

An old school friend of mine had a boyfriend who was a builder and in the late stages of the build, he also came over to work. The building was now nearing completion. I was working on a colour scheme. Extraordinary help was given. I had a friend who was an antique dealer and I met up with him in Morecambe where, at the time, he had a country club. He had a lot of contacts and could introduce me to a friend of his who were prepared to let me buy carpet at cost price, plus Vat. My friend had, in store, a quantity of turquoise cane dining furniture that he had bought in a sale and not used. He let me have it at the price hat he paid for it. I had found some curtain material that I loved and had planned the dining room colour scheme around the colours in this fabric. Once again, everything was falling into place. All that I needed was found, without too much effort.

In an environment like this, it is very easy to become complacent. I managed to find all the kitchen equipment that we needed, second hand, also crockery. This had to go temporarily into store. Meanwhile, we got on with the painting. Carpets were laid, the kitchen tiled, flooring laid, the kitchen equipment was installed. With my husband, I agonized over creating a menu. There were so many dishes that he wanted to include and so we ended up with over a hundred. Gordon Ramsey would have been horrified!

However money was getting tight again. I had to tell my brother that I only had two weeks work left for him, we were now very near completion, we were also about to run out of money again and still needed to buy in food stock.

I had changed banks during the course of the renovation and approached the bank that I was now dealing with, for additional funds. Once again they were reluctant to lend on an unknown business. My mother came to the rescue, offering her house as security against a loan. There didn't seem to be any alternative, other than just giving up, so we went ahead.

Now we had to find staff. My husband seemed to have plenty of contacts and found an additional chef and also a waiter that were prepared to come to the Island to work.

All the building work now complete we took the car over to Manchester to collect our first employees and to order all the basic foods we needed from an Indian Wholesaler.

Our chef who I will call Mr S. was as thin as a stick and had a big black beard. He smoked a pipe and had an air of quiet thoughtfulness about him. The waiter was in his twenties, I will just call him M. Having picked up the two of them, and their luggage, the following morning, we then went to the cash and carry.

I was expecting my husband to take charge of the ordering but instead he left it entirely up to Mr S. I was surprised but felt that there was no point in saying anything. Mr S. seemed confident and also seemed to know exactly what to order. My husband hardly said a word. With the benefit of hindsight, I think that this was the start of the problems that were going to visit in the not too distant future. Still we completed the shopping and then drove to Liverpool and caught the afternoon ferry back to the Island. Mr S. was amazed at how rural the Island was. He wondered where all the population was that was going to visit the restaurant.

It was August and we planned to open on the 21st I had started advertising the imminent opening and had also arranged for a leaflet drop in the form of takeaway menu's for the North of the Island.

A week later, our wagon load of stock arrived. The newsagents had decided to vacate the end shop after I had renovated it for them. As it turned out, that was not such a bad thing as there was enough stock to fill it: sacks of rice, and spices, cloves, nutmegs, peppercorns and bay leafs; tubs of ghee, sacks of flour, packs of poppadoms, huge jars of chutneys. All this was stacked in the former newsagents' and the air was heavy with the scent of spice.

I busied myself with sorting out work permits for our two employees. For the time being, they were going to live in the flat with us and Douglas, and would have to share a room. The opening day was looming. Most of the money from the additional loan had been swallowed up and it was make or break time. Some additional local staff had to be found. We advertised for a kitchen porter and a waitress. A man applied for the post of kitchen porter. My husband told him it was a hard job. He replied that he had been a London cab driver and that had set him up to cope with anything. The waitress we took on was a young girl of eighteen. She did seem just right, which was just as well, as out of all the applicants she did seem to be the only one that was suitable. So we were set.

Chapter 25

On the 20th of August everybody worked at getting the kitchen and dining area ready for our opening the next day. My husband was busy with his area of the kitchen. He was the tandoori chef. Mr S was the pan chef. My brother had drawn a scale plan of the kitchen before the equipment was installed. He also drew, to scale, the equipment that we had bought so that we could work out the best layout. My husband got very frustrated with this and eventually gave up on it which left me to deal with it. I made it as logical as possible.

Unfortunately though, when it came to actually installing the pieces as laid out on the plan nothing would fit as it should. A measurement cleared the confusion as the kitchen turned out to be a metre narrower than it was supposed to be. Quite a lot of re-organising was necessary and some of the equipment we had bought would now not fit. Luckily though we still ended up with a reasonable kitchen. Mr S. was happy with it. My husband was just grumpy.

In view of the extra finance that had been necessary I had decided that I would have to take a wage starvation of £50 a week. I couldn't ask my husband to take a minimum wage as he had to repay the money loaned from his family. There was another reason that I thought that my husband should have a full wage, and that was because I didn't want him to think that he was being exploited, as he had been, in the past. His weekly salary therefore was in excess of £300 a week net. The other employees also had to have appropriate wages or they wouldn't want to stay. By now my husband had been given permission to live and work on the Isle of Man by the Manx Immigration Office. This arrangement would then be reviewed in 5 years time.

My husband and Mr S had been around in the preceding few days and opened accounts with various wholesalers.

The 21st of August arrived. It was a Wednesday. It seemed an idea to open mid-week rather than at the weekend and ease ourselves into the new situation. Meat and vegetables were delivered and my husband and Mr S set to work on preparing the basic foods for the evening. Beautiful smells wafted out from the kitchen. The tables were set up. We were ready, as ready as we could be. Money had all but run out and instead of a bar we had my old sewing table with a cloth on it. That was the counter for the time being. We were due to open at six, and were all in the restaurant at five.

The other bit of building work that we hadn't been able to tackle was the front of the building and so it remained in it's tatty original condition.

A few people had booked tables and I had put my plastic "Reserved" signs on them. A few more tables were taken up with people who walked in off the street. Some people rang for takeaway orders and again some came in off the street for takeaways. It was a reasonable start. The former London taxi driver who became our kitchen porter walked out early on the first evening. After that we had quite a succession of kitchen porters.

The food was really good. Mr S was a marvellous pan chef and the busier we got the more he liked it. My husband was a marvellous tandoori chef. Word soon got round and we got busier and busier. Before long, weekends were booked, up to three weeks in advance, with usually two sittings. The takeaway was equally busy with people driving for our food from all over the Island. A recording studio in Port Erin in the South of the Island would ring up for a takeaway order and then have it delivered by taxi. We rocketed past the original cash forecasts. I was able to have a bespoke bar made to replace my sewing table and the inside of the restaurant now looked inviting.

My relationship with my husband was breaking down rapidly. He was desperately concerned that I should show only half the takings, in order to cut down on the Vat bills. I told him that we couldn't do that, as it was very easy for the Vat office to calculate very accurately our turnover and then we would be liable for a heavy fine. He also wanted to tamper with the meters and wanted them to run in reverse from time to time. This is what his "cousin brothers" did, apparently. I wouldn't agree to that either. By the third week in September, my husband was so frustrated with me that he started threatening to resign and close the business down.

On Friday 27th September with the restaurant fully booked, he did not come down to work the lunchtime shift and said that he had no intention of working that evening. The waiter M. decided that the Island was not for him and gave notice to leave. That, in fact, was a relief. Our little waitress's boyfriend came to work in his place. We made quite a good team at the front, but there was no pleasing my husband and he continued to rant at me after the restaurant had closed. We needed additional help in the kitchen and one of his friends who had attended our wedding said he would come over and work for us for a while. Things calmed down a little bit.

My brother had initially liked the idea of staying on the Island but had decided to go back to Wiltshire. We arranged to rent his house for staff accommodation as the restaurant continued to be very busy. Mr S and Mr Singh moved in over there. A month later the aggravation from my husband was starting up again. I went to see my doctor and talked over the situation with her. She suggested I talk the matter over with a psychiatrist and see if some solution could be found. Oddly enough, I saw the same psychiatrist that had looked after me when I had had a breakdown in 1983. He said that I had made a remarkable recovery and was very sympathetic to the situation that I now found myself in. He suggested that a Punjabi interpreter should be found to talk to my husband and see if the tensions could be resolved. I was feeling a total wreck and moved into the spare room.

My husband was quiet and I had two restful nights. It was October when I first spoke to my doctor about the problems in the restaurant. Now it was November and there was still no sign of an interpreter to talk to my husband.

Chapter 26

I hadn't wanted to have a licence to sell alcohol. There was a pub across the road, and if customers hadn't brought their own alcohol they could go to the pub and buy what they wanted and bring it over. It made for good relations with the publicans, and generated a jolly lighthearted atmosphere in the restaurant with waiters bringing food to the tables and the customers bringing tray of drinks in from the pub. Whilst all this was going on, our Mortgagee suggested that we were missing out on considerable income by not selling wines, beers and spirits. My husband took up this idea and, under pressure, I applied for a licence. This was granted but it changed the atmosphere in the restaurant. It became less light hearted. The waiting staff, already under pressure to cope with the busy restaurant, now had to serve drinks. Furthermore a recession was looming and we couldn't afford any more staff. If anything, we would have to cut back. A week after I had moved into the spare room, I heard my husband come upstairs in the early hours. I could hear him pacing up and down. Moments later, the bedroom door crashed open and the light went on and my husband stood swaying and glaring at me.

"You bitch, fucking English bitch!""Bitch people!", he said, taking me by the throat and shaking me about a bit,

"I'm going to kill you.", he said.

I was so tired I really wasn't bothered.

"If you are going to kill me, get on with it or go away and let me go to sleep." I said

"No," he decided, "I'm going to kill you slowly. I'm going to cut you up and burn you in the tandoori oven."

My husband's friend that had come over to help was a temporary measure and we knew that he would have to go at some point. He could work both in the kitchen and as a waiter and so was a very valuable member of staff. We did need a full time Indian waiter and I put an advert in an Indian trade paper. My husband's friend spoke to anyone who enquired. A waiter was found who was not in the country illegally. His English was not too good but that was something that he wanted to work on and so Mr Singh came to join us and went to live with Mr S and the other Mr Singh. He turned out to be a delight. Conscientious, clean, respectful and reliable and took a pride in his work. He and Mr S and Mr Singh, between them, kept me sane. My husband found someone who liked the idea of becoming a trainee chef.

Time flies when you are busy. It certainly did. Somehow the winter passed and the spring of 1992 arrived. Friction had now built up between my husband and my son to the point where they were ready to come to blows and since neither would back down, I had to tell Douglas to go and find somewhere else to live, as this situation could not be allowed to continue. He was very bitter and accused me of choosing a stranger over family. This was far from the case. I had to try to keep the business going and the additional discord was not helping. So Douglas moved out, hating me. Part-time staff came and went. My husband had given up telling me to fiddle the books and the meters and the

Vat. Each evening at the end of business we would cash up. Every food bill payment would be checked off against the entries on the till roll. All monies were accounted for each evening and the float for the following day would be left downstairs. The restaurant would be vacuumed and the tables reset, ready for business the next day. All the washing up would be done and the kitchen hosed down and left spotless. The day's takings I would then take upstairs and put in a filing cabinet.

One evening, my husband suggested that the staff were dishonest and taking money. I showed him how we cashed up and how the money was all accounted for. For reassurance, I counted the money out in front of him, showed how it tallied with the till total and all the entries, and that all the food order invoices were also kept and assured him that the staff were honest. They were busy days and I would go and pay into the bank every two or three days. Sometimes, when I was sorting out the banking I would think that there was less than there should have been, but it never occurred to me to go through the whole lot again and all the respective slips. No-one had access to the filing cabinet other than my husband and myself. Sometimes my husband would be angry if I was sorting out the banking in an afternoon and would say that I shouldn't be doing this in Company time. It seemed an odd thing to say, but then he said a lot of odd things.

When we had opened proper for business I had opened two bank accounts. One was expressly for Vat money. I would calculate the amount of Vat in the money that was taken and pay it directly into the Vat account so that the money was always there when the bills were due.

On a new business it was possible to make a late annual return. The same accountant that had been helping us from the start prepared this late return. When it had been prepared and audited, he posted it for myself and my husband to sign. It showed a loss of around £10,000 which was put down to various depreciations. My husband understood that a loss had been declared and refused to sign the return, so I phoned the accountant and asked what I should do. He told me to sign it and post it back to him and that he would sort something out. No sooner had I put it in the post than my husband decided that he would sign it. So I rang the accountant and upon receiving it, he put it back in the post. Back it came, but when faced with it again my husband again became reluctant to sign it. I was about to send it back again when he suddenly changed his mind and decided he would after all. He did, I was so relieved that unfortunately it made me want to laugh. It was only a little laugh but enough I suspect to make my husband think that I had tricked him in some way. He lunged at me. I grabbed the form and envelope and rushed to the door. He tried to grab me again but I shook him off and raced to the Post Office which was around the corner, looking over my shoulder all the while, expecting to see him in pursuit. Breathless, I reached the sanctuary of the Post Office, my heart thundering in my chest. There was a long, winding queue and a woman on the row in front of me, who ran a boutique and had seen me come in, now turned and informed me that she had Perla underwear on sale at 70% off.

The last thing I needed. Finally I reached the front of the queue and posted my letter. I didn't want to go back to the flat, so I got in the car and drove to a layby out of town and slept for a while.

Chapter 27

A couple of times, during the course of all this drama of our life and business, the wife of Mr S. had come over for a short visit. She was a rotund, traditional Indian lady and when she came to stay, she would spend some time in the kitchen, helping to make samosas. This would usually be done in the afternoon. Another afternoon chore would be to pick through the dried herb, methi (fenugreek), to remove as many as possible of the leaf stems, which tended to look like insect legs. One evening, a customer had got very upset over what he thought was an insect leg in his meal. I took a little dried fenugreek to the table, in order to show the customer that although care was taken to remove as many of the stems as possible, a few would be missed.

It could all seem so normal and sane and friendly. Mr S. explained to me that his wife had been his uncle's widow and that his father had sent him over to England to marry her. They had a little girl of five, and then there was his step-daughter who was 20. I asked him how he had felt about the arrangement. He told me he just did as his father asked and didn't question the decision. Mr S. did not complicate his life. He had a modest bungalow in a nice area in Manchester and when he could, he liked to garden. That was his life and work and he didn't complain.

However, tensions were building up with my husband again. It was now summer in 1992. The recession was in evidence. Interest rates were falling. We had an overdraft at the bank of £8000 I had got in touch with our mortgagee to see if he would consider reducing the amount of interest we were paying on the mortgage. He was not prepared to consider lowering our rate of 16%.

My husband and Mr S. would usually take a rest in the afternoons. I still had Dusty, the Spaniel. Oliver had become ill and had died at the age of 13, before the restaurant opened.

A crisis was looming. There had been no further help from either the doctor or the psychiatrist. We were still awaiting help in the form of an interpreter able to speak Punjabi, to be able to try, to understand my husbands attitude, and hopefully resolve the issues he felt that he had, before it was too late.

On 23rd of May 1992 I had gone up on to the mountain for a walk with Dusty. On the way back, I picked up clothes from the dry cleaners and got back to the flat at 4.30 p.m. My husband was waiting in the flat, in a fury. He demanded to know where I had been, but before I could reply, he began to go berserk, throwing furniture about and swearing at me. He moved on from that and began pushing me around the room, before knocking me to the floor. But before he could do anymore, his friend Mr Singh intervened.

Our living room was above the bar area in the restaurant and, luckily for me, Mr Singh was directly below us in the bar. On hearing the shouting and the commotion he came up to see what was going on. Mr Singh asked my husband what he was doing, and told him that he must stop. Things calmed down immediately. Mr Singh advised that we must try to carry on. I began to pick things up.

I asked my husband what was wrong and he said, "Better my simple life before."

 I told him that if we didn't look after the business my mother might lose her home. I reminded him of all the help my family had given. To which he replied, "Fuck off your mother, fuck off your brother, fuck off your son, I no care about these people."

I rang my solicitor and told him what had happened. He was aware of the tensions and worried that the stage was arriving where my life might actually be in danger. He did not want me to stay in the flat that night with my husband and asked if I had any friends where I might spend the night. If not, he would give me the number of a women's shelter. I rang my friend Nicky, and spent the night on her sofa. When I told her what had happened she offered me the use of her flat in Castletown. She had gone to live with a boyfriend and was not using it at the time. I had, from time to time, spent a night at my mothers if things had been particularly bad. She would leave a key for me outside the cottage where she lived in Peel. I would go over there at times when my husband's ranting carried on into the early hours, just to get some rest. He would ring her up and say that he didn't know where his wife was.

So the nightmare continued. I know it was a nightmare for both of us but I had reached a point where self-preservation now had to take priority. My solicitor had instructed me from now on never to be alone in the building with my husband. I went to work in the morning the next day. Mr Singh was working in the dining room. My husband and Mr S were in the kitchen. I went into the flat and put clothes in a bag and put it in my car. Then everything ran as normal. The restaurant was like a train on a fixed track, it just kept on going.

For years I had been in touch with an old school friend. Both our first marriages had broken down. My friend suggested that we took a break and went on the holiday of a lifetime.

I thought this a wonderful idea and eventually we decided to go for a two week holiday to Kenya. My friend was well travelled and made all the arrangements. The holiday was to consist of a safari, followed by a week's beach holiday in Mombasa. I had a credit card with a full available balance and used that to pay for the holiday. We were going to go in a month's time.

I told my husband that I intended to take a holiday and who I was going with. He had met my friend and so that was alright. He said that he needed a holiday and we agreed that he could go when I got back. He arranged to leave for a six week break on the day I got back. I would be back after he left, and I had no desire to see him. He hadn't been back to India for over eight years. Mr Singh would stand in for me as manager whilst I was away and deal with the banking. I haven't made much mention of our trainee chef. He came from Leeds and had had quite a good education. His English was good and he could also stand in as a waiter, if the need should arise, which meant that when Mr Singh finally had to leave, Mr H would be able to take his place. I did find him rather conceited, unfortunately, and prone to be a bit cocky.

Chapter 28

The day of departure for my holiday finally arrived. I spent the night at my mother's and went by taxi to the Airport the next morning. I hadn't travelled much at all. In fact I had only been to Eire. I was meeting my friend at Gatwick in the afternoon, and was really looking forward to the break. My friend was one of those beautiful people who never seemed to have a weight problem, had a figure to die for and was supremely confident. I felt gauche and naïve and frumpy in comparison. We managed to find each other and a place to sit and wait for our flight. It was a long flight and the plane was packed with holiday makers, not the most enjoyable experience I have ever had. We arrived at Mombasa Airport the next day and were transported to the hotel where we were to spend one night before going on to Niarobi for another night, before being taken to the first of the Safari lodges that we would be staying in.

Five nights were spent in Safari lodges, the days spent being driven around, hoping for glimpses of the animals we expected to see. I think it was the rest that I needed more than anything. The Safari over, we were taken back to Niarobi. We were to go back to Mombasa on an overnight train and so we had a little time to look around the town. It was a shock for me to see how run down it was with the broken pavements and forlorn shops with their neglected and crumbling facades. The beggars on the streets, lepers who had been carried in to sit and beg during the day, would be taken home at night.

The afternoon passed and we made our way back to the hotel where our luggage had been left until we would be taken to catch the train later on. I think that train journey was possibly the highlight of the holiday for me. A steam train pulled into the station and we boarded it and settled into a compartment. It was so old fashioned, like something one would see in an Agatha Christie film. There were bunks that pulled out to sleep on. In the dining room white clad waiters served up a silver service dinner. The dining carriage was lit by gas lamps that flickered and cast an uneven amber light. The scene could have been set 60 years earlier. The train rocked, as it rhythmically made its way through the night. We retired to our compartment and settled down for the night. I was still taking sleeping tablets, it was so nice to sleep.

Daylight came and we opened the blind. We sped past fields of sisal, mud hut villages, children had come to wave at the passing train. We threw coins from the window for them and some clothing. Breakfast was served in the dining carriage and by lunchtime we were back in Mombasa. We were taken to the beach hotel where we were to spend the rest of our holiday. It was lovely. We took baths and relaxed. But the restaurant was never far from my mind.

There was something else as well. My friend and I seemed to have grown in different directions, something seemed to be lacking, or maybe it was our complicated personal lives that clouded the experience. The holiday finally came to an end. I had lost a load of weight and felt great and was even looking forward to going home.

Everytime I needed to cash a travellers cheque I had had to produce my passport. By mistake, the last time that I had cashed a cheque, I had left my passport in the office. On the morning that we were due to leave, I couldn't find my passport and then it occurred to me where it would be. The matter became complicated as it had been locked in the safe. The manager had the key and wasn't coming in until later. My friend had wanted us to be among the first to leave the hotel, to ensure that we would be seated on the plane together. Frantic phone calls were made to the manager and eventually he arrived and I got my passport, but we were among the last to leave the hotel and now guaranteed not to be sitting together. My friend was angry with me and set out to make me feel thoroughly miserable. We waited in silence to board the plane.

Back in London though, we said our goodbyes and promised to keep in touch. I got the coach back to Heathrow and from there the flight for the Isle of Man. I got a taxi to my friend's flat, collected my clothes and drove to Ramsey, in time for the evening's business. I would stay in the restaurant flat while my husband was away.

The oppressive atmosphere in the restaurant had gone, along with my husband. I felt very welcome and it was a pleasure to work. I had promised my husband that I would pay his wages into the bank each week, since it hadn't been possible to give him a lump sum. The weeks went by, there was a happy atmosphere at work. The staff began to say that they would like to leave when he came back. That was how I felt too.

About halfway through his break, I got a call from the Vat Office saying that they would like to do a spot check. This was common practice with a new business and I was totally confident that everything would be in order since I had been meticulous about keeping records. A few days later, a lady inspector arrived and I handed her all the sales slips and till rolls. She settled herself at the dining table at the flat which doubled up as my office and began her work. She would arrive in the morning and stay all day. For three days she worked, reconciling every entry on the till roll with every sale slip.

Eventually she asked if she could have a word with me. She said that there was a discrepancy. I replied that I had been very careful. She suggested that I sat down.

"How much is it? "I asked.

She told me that there were undeclared monies of over eight thousand pounds. Vat would have to be paid on this money and there would also be a fine. At this, my mind went spinning back over the previous eighteen months, my husband only wanting me to show half the takings and then after a while, not going on about it anymore, his annoyance if he found me doing the banking in the flat in the afternoon. I reckoned that if he had taken between £20 and £30, a day that would add up to the money that was not accounted for. I remembered the feeling I had, from time to time, when I had thought that there should have been more to pay in. I also had a pretty good idea of whose instruction he would have been following, if my suspicions were correct.

The officer said that they would be writing to me concerning this, to confirm the undeclared monies.

Chapter 29

This, on top of everything else, was too much. It took a few days to sink in. Meanwhile, a letter arrived from my husband, written for him by someone who was able to write in English. He was enjoying his break, he missed me, his mother hoped one day to meet her daughter-in-law. I didn't want him to come back. I phoned his brother in Nottingham and told him that his brother, my husband, had been stealing money and that I was so fed-up I could no longer carry on with this. His brother insisted that he (his brother) would not have taken money. I told him that there was no other explanation and that I would no longer stand by my husband. I told his brother to keep him away from the Island and that if he caused me anymore trouble I would divorce him without hesitation.

A few days later, I went to see my solicitor and told him about recent developments and what I suspected. He wanted to get the fraud squad involved to investigate. But, I stopped short of this and said, instead, that I had stopped my husband from returning to the Island and the money should just be written off. In truth, I had begun to wonder how much more I could take and was afraid of pushing myself into another breakdown. The first one had been a terrifying experience and I did not know if I could cope with another. I was not prepared to take that risk. Besides, I had to keep working whilst I endeavoured to sort out the muddle that was my personal life.

Understandably,my husband was livid. He went to stay with his buddy in Scotland, and had now managed to get legal aid to claim his share of the property that he owned jointly with me. He had no trouble signing the forms confirming his claims. One of which was the amount of £25,000 he had borrowed from friends and family when we had been running short of funds during the setting up of the restaurant. However, since he had probably had in the region of £30,000 over eighteen months, I did not feel that this was a legitimate claim. He had no demands on his income. The company paid the mortgages both to our private mortgagee and to the bank, in respect of the charge against my mothers property. It also paid rates and power bills. It was up to him to repay any monies owed out of his income. However he did not see it this way.

I petitioned for divorce now, on the grounds that my husband had behaved in such away that I could not reasonably be expected to live with him. And so we were was divorced on the 15th March 1993.

Less than a month later, I reverted to my maiden name of Lobb. I could not associate myself with my former husband in any way shape nor form and I certainly did not want to use his name. Now I had been "Ratcliffe" when I was adopted by my step-father, "Richardson" by my first marriage, "Ram" by my second marriage, and now I had come full circle and was "Lobb" again.

The recession continued to have an effect, with business slowing down. Interest rates were now plummeting and people were cutting back on luxuries, of which eating out was one. Trade was slowing down. Once again, I approached my mortgagee about re-negotiating the interest paid on the loan and again, he would not entertain the idea.

A new development was about to present itself. The step daughter of Mr S. was of a marriageable age and wanted to get married. Mr S., as was the custom, set about finding a suitable man to import to become her husband. This involved making phone calls all over the place. He was a careful man, and the cost of this was huge, particularly as calls were made from a public phone box. He had been told that if, when he had been connected to the number he was calling, instead of feeding coins into the phonebox, he were to lower a coin on a bent piece of wire the connection would be made and he could retrieve his coin and use it over and over again. What his advisor didn't tell him or didn't know, was that every time a fraudulent call is made, a special code appears on the phone records, giving the time of the call, the length of the call, the number called and the location of the phone box from where the call was made. Mr S. was in the habit of making his wedding arrangement calls before he came to work in the mornings, always from the same phone box and always around the same time.

When business was brisk, when the restaurant first opened, I had bought a little van, and used this to go and collect supplies from the wholesalers. This morning I had been into Douglas and got back. The staff had seen the van pull up and were waiting for me at the front of the restaurant. There was obviously something wrong. They told me that Mr S. had been arrested and that the Police wanted me to go to the station when I got back. I hadn't far to go, as it was only two doors away. I thought it would be something minor that would be sorted out quickly. Not so, as it happened. The phone company, on becoming aware of the regular fraudulent calls being made, had contacted the police, who, in turn, had stationed some plain clothed police officers near the phone box from where Mr S. had made his calls. As regular as clockwork, Mr S. had turned up and started his calls and had promptly been arrested.

In the station, they had taken his pocket book off him and all the fraudulent calls that had been made matched the numbers in it. Yet he denied making the calls. I was asked if I would like to talk to him. I did, but despite explaining to him how he had come to be arrested, I couldn't get him to admit to what he was accused of doing, and so he was taken to the Police station in Douglas and put in a cell. Luckily we still had Mr Singh with us. The trainee chef had now had to work at the tandoori dishes proper and Mr Singh did the curries. But Mr Singh would be leaving after the daughter of Mr S. was married.

The next day, I went to see Mr S. in the police station in Douglas. Mr S. used to call me "Basanti." He still denied the charge.

He said "Basanti, it's very peaceful here. The policemen are bringing me tobacco for my pipe, my wife isn't phoning and I am happy."

Not what I wanted to hear.

Chapter 30

This situation could not remain unchanged and I had to arrange a solicitor for him. The solicitors' was becoming like my second home. I seemed to be calling on them every week for one matter or another. The solicitor came with me to see Mr S. He was clearly very content and had no intention of making a confession. I was becoming frantic. It was not possible to run the restaurant without him. I visited him the next day and there was still no change in his attitude. I went for a third time.

He said "Basanti, what would you like me to do?"

"Please, just tell them the truth," I said.

Finally, he said that he would, I rang the solicitors, his solicitor came out and dealt with the paperwork and I took him back to work.

Normality could resume. But we needed another chef as there was no-one to cover if either Mr S. or Mr H. wanted a break or were ill. Mr S. had many contacts and said that he would make some phone calls and see if there was a chef who would like to come and work over here. I reminded him to check that their paperwork was in order, as I was not prepared to employ anyone who was in the country illegally. A chef was found and I went to pick him up from the airport. He seemed quite competent and so Mr H. could take a break.

The overdraft at the bank still stood at £8000. There was £8000 in the Vat account. We had a new bank manager and the atmosphere in the bank was noticeably cooler. Interest rates were now down to around 5% and we were still paying 16%. The day after the new chef Abdul arrived, I asked to see his papers, passport etc and explained that I needed them in order to apply for a work permit. He said that they were with his brother in England and that he would get them sent over. Days later, there was still no sign of these papers arriving. He now said that his brother was a travelling salesman and was away from home a lot, and that he had promised that they would be sent on as soon as he had time to look for them.

I think I could win prizes for being naive, gullible etc. I got in touch with the work permits office and asked them what I should do. It had occurred to me that there might be some temporary arrangement that might be available until the illusive documents could be found. The Immigration Officer asked me to take him in as they would like to question him. It didn't take them long to work out that he was in the country illegally. He was told that on no account must he do any work. At this he became angry and challenged the officers decision. He was told that he had two choices, either he could stay in my staff accommodation, but not work or they could put him in prison. He was asked how much money he had in the bank and told to use all of this if necessary to get the first flight that he could back to Saudi Arabia, which was, apparently, where he had originally come from.

He did actually still have a passport and a few days later, I took him to book his flight. He would be leaving in a week's time. He told me that he had a wife in Saudi Arabia and when he left for a visit to the U.K his wife was pregnant. He came on a holiday visa, but then liked it here and had been encouraged to forget his wife and stay and so he too had become swallowed up by the black market. He told me that he was advised to try to get married to an English woman, in order to be able to stay in the country.

The day of his departure eventually arrived and I went to pick him up to take him to the airport. I was expecting a rather unpleasant journey, since I was responsible for getting him deported. But I got a pleasant surprise when he said that he was very grateful to me for what had happened, and was looking forward to seeing his wife again and his daughter who was now 2 years old. He said that he intended to open a taxi business when he got back.

Chapter 31

The daughter of Mr S. duly got married. Mr Singh left us and went back to Scotland. Work in the restaurant settled down again. Mrs S. came to visit with the youngest daughter and the now married daughter and her husband. The husband was quite a glamorous creature with lots of gold jewellery. They stayed for a few days. The new husband had been found work in a factory and would start work after the visit.

The year was grinding on. My visits to the solicitors' continued. It had been suggested to my former husband, via his solicitors, that he sign the restaurant and property over to me and that I would take over the debts. The response was that I should just sign everything over to him and that he would take over the debts. I couldn't do that.

In the autumn, Mr S. took me to one side and said that he had a problem. He told me that his son-in-law was lazy and did not want to work and he was going to have to go back to find work nearer to home so that he could, "Give this man a kick." He said that before he left, he would teach me to cook. He was only too aware of my problems and said that at least if I could cook, I would not need to pay another chef. I felt sick at the prospect. I would have three weeks to learn what Mr S. had been doing for over 20 years and that was already familiar to him as it was the traditional food that he was used to. But it would save a lot of money and the other Mr Singh was very efficient at the front of the restaurant. First though, I needed to get to grips with the tandoori oven, and I needed Mr H.. to get more confident with the curries. I had a little note book and made many notes, detailing everything that I thought would help me. I learned to make the naan bread dough, and the marinades for the meats to be cooked in the tandoori oven. I also felt sick with nerves. I still had to master the curries and Mr S. was determined that I would learn. He all but chained me to the cooker. I made more notes. Every little detail I wrote down in a little red book.

Douglas had come back to live in the flat. So many things had happened whilst he had lived in his world and me in mine. He had fallen in love and produced two grandchildren for me. When I had told him that I was not ready to be a grandmother. He told me that life did not wait for me to be ready. Sadly, though, his relationship had failed.

The three weeks passed and Mr S., who had been my rock, was leaving. All I had was my little red note book and my head crammed full of Indian cooking. Mr S. left. I was traumatised by the thought of what now lay ahead. I asked Mr H.. to deal with the curries on that first night, as he had more experience. It was a Saturday. What an initiation! I ended up with severe burns on both arms from putting the naan breads into the tandoori oven. But, somehow, we got through it. The evening eventually came to an end and we cleared up and closed up. At that time, we still opened 7 days a week.

The next day, I wondered how on earth I was going to manage to bear the heat from the oven when I had to reach in and put the naan breads on the hot clay sides. Then I had a brain wave and bought some elastic tubular bandages and put those over my burnt arms and so I coped and Mr H.. coped. And the staff coped in the dining room. In that respect, I was very lucky.

However more change was on the way. Takings were down. My mortgagee now decided that the front of the building, which remained in it's tatty state, was putting people off coming in and insisted that something should be done about it. When I said that I was struggling to make ends meet as it was, he said that he would pay for the work and would extend the period over which the mortgage was repaid. And so work began. There were huge wooden lintels over the large windows and on closer inspection these turned out to be rotten. It was a big job, getting them replaced and, at one point, it looked as though the whole of the front of the building was about to fall away. It didn't. New lintels were put in and the front of the building was covered in wooden panelling. The husband of one of the waitresses painted it and it looked very smart. However it didn't make the slightest bit of difference to business.

It was now 1994. Douglas had begun to help in the kitchen and had picked up the tandoori cooking very quickly. I decided to send Mr H.. on a management course at the local college but it had a disastrous effect on his already large ego and he became unmanageable. I had given him an increase in wages when he had to take on more responsibility in the kitchen, but now I was beginning to realise that he was a luxury that I couldn't afford, that, coupled with his attitude, made me realise that I would have to let him go.

I decided to try to let him down gently and asked if he would like to go out to lunch the following day, which was Sunday. We no longer opened on Sundays. He liked the idea of that, so I booked a table at a nice restaurant in a different part of the Island. He turned up for this treat looking unwashed and unshaved. In the restaurant, I felt so uncomfortable with what I was about to do, I couldn't sit still and squirmed constantly in my seat. We had our main course and he looked disdainfully around the restaurant, being highly critical of everything. Then he asked what was up with me. I told him that I hadn't brought him out for the good of his health and dropped my bombshell. He started making strange gulping noises and I, being relieved of the pressure wanted to laugh. I managed not to. Instead I asked him if he would like a dessert. He declined and I called for the bill. Horrors! I had forgotten my cheque book and hadn't got any money with me and he ended up paying the bill.

He left. Now I had to face my demon and become the pan chef. I was terrified. Douglas became the tandoori chef. How lucky was I with Douglas. He picked up the skill of the tandoori cooking very quickly, as though he had been born to it. But I could only pay him a minimum wage, like me, £50. a week.

Business was still deteriorating, but I knew it was nothing to do with the quality of the food. I knew we had got that right. I bumped into a few customers on the street and they said that the place just wasn't the same without me at the front. That surprised me. I didn't think that I counted that much. I explained that I had had to take over the cooking and that there was nothing that I could do about it. We missed a mortgage payment. I went to the bank manager to see if there was anyway that he was prepared to help me. He wasn't. Quite the reverse, he said that I must use the money in the Vat account to pay off the overdraft. I did that. Then I couldn't pay the Vat bills and had to pay those by instalments. I was now working a hundred hours a week, starting around 8 in the morning and finishing around 2 the following morning. I would never leave the kitchen until it was spotless and Mr Singh kept the dining room immaculate. I was starting to have difficulty paying suppliers.

I went to the solicitors' and suggested that it seemed the only way out would be to try to sell the property. He put this to my former husband's solicitors. My ex-husband was against this and we ended up having a court hearing in order to make him see that there was no alternative. So the property was advertised for sale but the only interest came from time wasters. Meanwhile another mortgage payment was missed. My solicitor suggested that really I had nothing left to lose if I were to give the buildings and business to my former husband. And so it was offered to him. He said he no longer wanted it. Another mortgage payment was missed.

Summer was approaching. Douglas had mastered the art of blending spices and could now produce delicious curries. We decided to take a risk and take on a local person to train as a tandoori chef. This would enable me to go back to the front of the restaurant. So Terry joined us, all 6' 7" of him. He had attended the local college and done a catering course. He towered over everyone, and despite tears and tantrums with the occasional walkout after a spat with Douglas, he mastered the tandoori cooking. I went back to the front of the restaurant, but it was a strain. I couldn't afford to give Douglas the salary that he was more than worthy of and yet he persevered.

However there were now four destructive elements in place. Namely, the money which I had absolutely no doubt had been taken by my then husband, the Vat money that had been demanded by the bank to clear the overdraft, leaving me in a fix trying to pay Vat bills by instalments, the mortgage which was still at an inflexible 16% and the recession, now very much in evidence.

A third mortgage payment was missed and my mortgagee phoned me one evening. There had been no interest in the property from serious buyers, and he wanted to have it sold by Coroner's Auction. I had to decide on a date for our last trading day, and settled on Saturday September 17th (1994) which was about six weeks away. I called a staff meeting and explained what was going to happen, and why, and when, and said that anyone who felt that they would prefer to go and find alternative employment should do so, as there would be no guarantees regarding wages now. Only Mr Singh chose to leave, which was entirely understandable. What was surprising was that the rest chose to stay.

Our final trading day arrived, and our stalwart regulars came to say their goodbyes. It was a painful day. The next day, we cleaned the place until it shone. The tiles, the extractors, the fridges, freezers, everything was left in immaculate order. I hoped that it might help the sale. Furthermore I managed to pay the staff, we scraped through with just £30 left over. I had been moved by their loyalty. It had been above and beyond the call of duty. One of the waitresses offered to take Dusty. She was very fond of her and I let her go, thinking she would be better off.

Chapter 32

By now, the Coroner was involved. He was, in fact, very understanding and let me take my time sorting the flat out. I sold most of the furniture, wardrobes, beds etc and used the money to live on temporarily. Not wanting to leave, I slept on a couple of rolled up duvets on the living room floor. I managed to hang on until almost the end of October. The Coroner had been remarkably patient but he had called and told me that he really did need to change the locks. He urged me to take anything that I wanted from the restaurant. It was kind, but I hadn't the heart to even go in there and so left everything. Again, I thought it might help the sale if everything looked pristine.

I still had the estate car which I had taken on, on a lease arrangement, another one of my follies, though as usual, I had had the best of intentions. As the full time live in staff were passing driving tests, it seemed like a good idea, at the time to have a safe reliable car for them to use. I was going to go and stay with my mother. When the day came for me to finally leave, I put the few belongings I had in the car, handed the keys in to the Coroner, and left.

I didn't get a warm welcome at my mother's. I think we were both very uncomfortable. I hoped that it would be a temporary situation and that the auction would clear any outstanding debts and leave me with enough, hopefully, to buy a small property and make a new start. The auction was to take place on November 17th. I couldn't bring myself to go and spent the day sitting and hoping. About 4 p.m I phoned the Coroner. He told me that the property had only realised £82,000 two thousand pounds less than it had been for sale for, in it's semi-derelict condition, before the recession, despite having in excess of £140,000 invested in rebuilding the ground floor area. The mortgagee had decided to cut his losses, since he had first claim on the proceeds and settle for the balance, after costs and not chase me for mortgage arrears. He died six weeks after he got his money.

This news was mentally poleaxing for me. I felt stunned. I gave my mother the devastating news but beyond that, I wasn't capable of speech. The following day, I had begun to slip into a deep depression. I don't think the full enormity of the situation that we now found ourselves in, had fully registered with my mother, or maybe it had. Our relationship rapidly grew tensions. I couldn't shake off the shock reaction to the news that I had had from the Coroner and would sit in a chair, stunned. My mothers reaction to this was unfortunate.

"Look at you!" she sneered, "You will never do anything!"

My mother, like Douglas's father, had a tendency to say something devastating at a "key" wrong moment. Years later, I chanced on some literature which drew attention to a condition called "Alexithymia" from the Greek - a for "lack", lexis for "word" and thymos, for "emotion", a very sad aspect of a person's inability to express their feelings, which can, understandably, have a devastating effect on another person.

I was to mention this to Douglas's father, years later, when we met up again. I was astonished, that, for once, I got an intelligent reply. He said that he thought that a lot of people would have this problem. I told him that it was possible to resolve the problem (which apparently is thought to develop in childhood) and that help was available in the form of training and teaching, to help people to develop the emotions that they lack. I even thought that maybe all our problems could be resolved and that we might achieve that 'happy ever after' after all. Except that, his response to that was that no-one likes to admit that they have a problem, especially not one of this kind. With that, he "ran away" from the knowledge, and I gave up on pursuing it further.

To my mother's comment, I replied, "You don't know what I'll do."

Although all that appealed to me at that time was walking over Peel Hill and flinging myself over the cliffs and on to the rocks below. The only thing that stopped me was the same thing that always stopped me, the thought of Douglas.

However, there was a huge problem, and that was that my mother's house had been held as security against the business. About a third of the loan had been paid off but there was still the outstanding amount. I raised the subject. I had started looking in the papers and there were some very cheap mortgages available. It seemed that my mother just wanted to give up and let the bank repossess the property and let things take their course. I convinced her to reconsider. She didn't want my name on the deeds, though, and she wasn't interested in a low interest mortgage over a longer period. She wanted it paid off quickly. We went to the bank and she was given a mortgage to which we were both to contribute. Somehow, it seemed to have escaped her that, at the time, I had no income and on top of that, I was now being chased for money, via the Coroner, by my creditors.

She was a marvellous baker and was always baking something. I comforted myself, gorging on delicious scones, cakes and bread. I became very ill, almost unable to breathe. It was assumed that the cause was the stressful years I had had, followed by the devastating shock of losing all. My legs and feet filled with fluid and I was aware of lumps in my breasts. It was painful to walk upstairs. I thought, with relief, that I would die and that death would release me. I had never thought of death with fear and had only ever thought of it as a release. But I didn't die and ended up going to the doctor for something to relieve my breathing difficulties. Inhalers did not seem to be working. I was still taking sleeping pills, so I did manage to sleep. I was put on steroids. The doctor didn't make any enquiries about my eating habits which had been subject to a massive shift since losing the restaurant and I was now well on the way to becoming a vegetarian, something that I had always liked the idea of.

The steroids were making me feel fantastic. I began looking for work and found a part-time job in a little supermarket in Douglas. Sometimes I would catch the bus in. If I was short of money I would hitch hike or cycle (the lease car had been repossessed). People got used to seeing me hitching and I didn't have much

Difficulty getting lifts. One day, the man who ran the tailors' business in the town picked me up. Whilst we were chatting, he asked if I could sew. He said that perhaps I could make a bit more money helping with doing sewing alterations. I had had useful experience at the Gents' Outfitters and would be able to help with sales in the shop as well. He asked if I had some garment that I had made, that I could take in. I did that and fortunately the work was to a high enough standard for me to be trusted with alterations. So that was a bit more income. I had brought a few pieces of furniture from the flat. An old chesterfield sofa, some pine furniture and an oil painting. At that time, on the local radio station, there was a slot where people would write or phone in with items they would like to swop and what they would like in exchange. I wrote in, and offered my pieces of furniture and the oil painting,in exchange for a car. I would have been more than happy with a Robin Reliant but was actually offered a Ford Capri. What a fabulous car! I loved it and now I could go and visit Dusty who was in the North of the Island. My former waitress was not having an easy time with her, she seemed to be fretting and her condition worsened as the weeks went by. Eventually, I brought her back to Peel and, in time, she settled down and became my happy, wilful little dog again.

Chapter 38

Now that I had a car, I had more flexibility. I wondered if there would be any market for the Indian starters that I used to make at the restaurant. I managed to find a few outlets, prepared to sell them and would cook a batch at the weekends and deliver them. I also found there was interest from people wanting Indian dinner parties.

Some years before, my mother had been on a course to learn how to do picture framing. She had always been artistic and thought it would be nice to be able to frame her paintings herself. She had no difficulty picking up the skill and turned what was the dining room into a picture framing room, set up, at some cost, with picture framing equipment. Since she was a member of a painting group, it wasn't only her own paintings she ended up framing, but those of other members of the group as well, and this, at cost. Word gets around and more and more people found their way to her rickety cottage, perched on the edge of the broughs.(broughs, is the steep, high, bank that sloped down to the fishyards)

I came in one day and among the work that had come in to be framed was a rather lovely charcoal study of a young woman looking at a ring on her finger, presumably, an engagement ring. I asked whose work it was and was told that it had been done by someone who had been an art teacher but who had given up his job in order to devote his time to painting. He now just worked part-time in the woodworking business across the road, to help to make ends meet.

We have a beautiful theatre in Douglas, designed by Frank Matcham. On Saturday mornings, friends of the theatre would give guided tours around the building. I decided some weeks later that this might be a nice change and so decided to hitch hike into Douglas and have the tour and learn more about the theatre. My car needed a repair and was off the road for a few days. I had £5 in my purse but was reluctant to spend it unless I absolutely had to. I walked a good few miles before I started hitching, just for the exercise.

A car stopped and I got a lift into Douglas. I got into conversation with the driver, as one does. I found him very attractive, though I tried not to think about it too much. He asked where I lived and it transpired that he was the artist that had done the charcoal sketch that I had so much admired. He said that he usually painted very large pictures and that my mother had banned him from bringing these in, as they were too big for her to manage in her cramped framing room. He said he had another charcoal sketch in the boot of his car and asked if I would like to see it. I said that I would love to! So when we got to Douglas, he showed it to me. It was actually quite ghastly, a life drawing of a particularly gaunt and scrawny man. However, I managed to make appreciative noises and then went off for my theatre tour.

I was the only person that turned up and was given star treatment by the people who arranged the tours. I was shown around every fascinating area of the theatre and given the background history. This was rounded off by tea and scones, just for me. I felt like a Queen. Very conspicuous by its presence, was the "Friends of the Gaiety" donation box. There wasn't a charge for the tour and being the only one there, I felt obliged to put something in the box. They had all been so very nice I felt that I couldn't ask them to give me change for my £5 note and so I put it in, thanked them for a marvellous tour and left to hitch hike back to Peel.

After the day when the "artist" had given me a lift, our paths seemed to cross on a regular basis. Some weeks later, my car was being serviced by a mechanic who also had a workshop across the road. I was due to go to work at the Grocer's at 1 p.m that day and went to get my car. I was sure that I had told the mechanic that I needed it but he wasn't there and the workshop was locked up, with my car inside. I was just coming away from peering through the workshop windows, when the "artist" appeared. On hearing of my plight, he offered to lend me his car for the afternoon, saying that I could drop the key through the letter box when I got back from work, as he would have gone out. I thought about him all afternoon. I was becoming infatuated. I wrote him a little poem, describing my plight and his subsequent kindness.

And then I did something very bold and added another note

asking if he would like to accompany me on the last ferry day trip of the season to Liverpool. When I got back to Peel, I put the poem and the note together with the car key in an envelope and went to put it through his letter box. He was, however, still in and came to the door before I had finished pushing my envelope through. I was invited into his enchanting cottage. I explained that I had put a note in the envelope and waited whilst he read it. There was a moments hesitation before he said that, "Yes," he would like to go with me on the day trip.

Meanwhile, I had decided that I needed to earn more money and had applied for waitressing work in an Italian restaurant in Douglas. I was due to start work there the Saturday after the day trip to Liverpool. It meant giving up the tailoring work and I would have to stop my side line of weekend sales of India starters and dinner parties.

By now, I was counting the hours to the much anticipated day trip, which fell on September 16th 1995. We had to leave quite early in the morning, and, because we didn't really know each other very well, we gabbled a lot of nonsense on the way over. We went to the Walker Art Gallery, wandered around the old town and had a wonderful day. A dangerous day for me as I had become totally smitten. As it turned out he apparently felt the same about me and when we were only minutes away from Douglas harbour he asked if I fancied prolonging the evening and going to see a play. I'd actually seen the play only the previous evening but the opportunity of spending a few more hours in his company was irresistible and I told him that I would love to!

The next day was Sunday and I was working in the Grocer's

in the morning. He had asked if I would like to go for a walk in the afternoon. I loved walking so I said I'd love to go. That evening I cooked him a vegetarian Indian meal in his cottage. He didn't want me to leave, I didn't want to leave, but I did. Only to go and live with him a week later. By this time, I was head over heels in love and he seemed to feel the same.

I couldn't believe it. Somebody loved me, despite the fact that I wasn't solvent. He told anyone that had an ear that I was the love of his life. How many of us though, manage to see ourselves through the other person's eyes? We meet someone whose company we really enjoy and who seems to reciprocate those feelings. My boyfriend had met me when I was really down on my luck. We did seem to have a lot of common interests. I am very practical and a good cook. He enjoyed my adulation of him as an "Artist". What he didn't know was that I was also capable of being creative. Besides, I do seem to have an uncanny knack of screwing things up and this was to prove no exception. And so I found myself head over heels in love. Or was I? I always made it clear that I was not a great fan of pub culture, but I was to find out that it is quite extraordinary the lies that a man will tell.

Chapter 39

I began my new job at the Italian restaurant and worked the lunchtime shift and five evenings, and apart from Saturday evening. I found myself in a situation where I was the only member of staff waiting on. I had to seat customers, take meal orders, serve meals, take drink orders, serve drinks,take dessert orders, serve desserts, clear tables, reset tables, serve coffee, and make out bills and as the restaurant filled up these duties would all become tangled up with one another and become chaotic.

My employer would be shouting for me to take food out, customers would be trying to catch my attention for extra wine, coffee, desserts, bills. It could get nightmarish.

I would get home around midnight exhausted. My partner would be waiting up for me and would have lovingly prepared some little delicacy for me to eat. Which, in truth, was the last thing I wanted. A few weeks into the relationship, he confessed that there was something that he had not hitherto mentioned. He was supposed to go on a week's holiday with his sister and her husband and a woman friend of his sister's. Hmmm. He said that now he felt that he didn't want to go without me and would ask his sister if it would be alright if I came along too. It was okayed. The arrangement was made and I did manage to arrange to take a week off work. The holiday season had ended and the restaurant was a bit quieter. The boss's son would stand in for me, with a bit of extra help. So I was going on a holiday and going to meet the sister, who did sound quite formidable, and her husband, who apparently had been an M.P for the Green Party, and the sister's friend who had been her head mistress when she had been doing her training to teach teachers how to teach. The former headmistress was now a school inspector.

We took my car and drove to Scotland, arriving at his sister's house in the early evening. The friend swooped up to my boyfriend and said, in a very dramatic way, "We meet at last!"

She clearly was very taken with him. She was also a high earner and apparently owned a beautiful cottage.

The next day we all piled into a car that had been hired

for the trip and set off to the far North of Scotland. I was beginning to feel surplus to requirements, despite still being the centre of my boyfriend's attention. We booked into the centre where we were to spend the next three nights and after an evening meal and chatting we all turned in. We were going to do lots of walking over the next two days. During the evening meal, the previous day, I had sat next to my boyfriend. The following morning at breakfast, his sister decided that it was time to separate us and placed me at the head of the table and my boyfriend at the far end, next to her friend. That I was considered unsuitable was unmistakable. The two days passed and the experience was forgotten.

I went back to work. Christmas came and went and Spring came. I was still run ragged at the restaurant and began to dread the approach of the holiday season and particularly T.T fortnight, as the restaurant was guaranteed to be very busy. I suspected too much was going to be expected of me.

I was beginning to have a problem with my teeth and eventually had to visit a dentist. I had not been to a dentist for years, aside from the fact that I hated visiting the dentist in the first place. The last one that I saw in Ramsey had informed me that my jaw bone was being re-absorbed by my body and that my teeth would become loose and fall out. Now I had to go though. I was recommended a lady dentist in Douglas and made an appointment. She was wonderfully sympathetic to my paranoia of dentists. My teeth were in poor shape and I had several abscesses forming on my top jaw. She asked if there were any health issues that I knew of. I told her, that when I had had to have a medical, prior to taking out life assurance for the mortgage on the restaurant

I was found to have a heart murmur, and that I also suffered from asthma and took sleeping pills. I was now visiting the dentist almost every week and had to take a sachet of Amoxicillin before each visit. With each abscess, I lost another tooth.

I also began to dread any visits that my boyfriend's sister and her husband made to the Island. I really did not fit in. Peel boasted a Health Food shop which had been run by various individuals over the years. At one point, two of my mother's friends had run it and she would go and help out. They worked at it for quite a few years before selling the business to two young married women who, in turn, built it up quite a bit, before they too, decided that they would like to sell it as a going concern and move on. However, they were not so lucky and no interested party turned up to buy it, and so they decided that they had no choice but to sell off the stock and close it down. Which they did, but then still had quite a residue of stock left. I began to wonder about this and mentioned the possibility of re-opening it to my boyfriend. He was most enthusiastic and said that he had always fancied running a shop like that. I approached the girls with my notion and they were delighted with the idea and worked out a price for the remaining stock. My mother lent me £1,500 to buy basic new stock, in order to re-open the shop.

I gave my notice at the restaurant and came out with a little extra money in the form of holiday pay. This enabled me to buy some wood for shelving, which my boyfriend installed. We re-registered the business, with us as joint partners and the shop re-opened for business on April 1st 1996. It was a much calmer life and my health began to settle down again. Very little income, though. My boyfriend would help in the shop on Saturdays. He had a very proprietorial presence and quite a few people assumed that it was his shop and that I was merely working for him. Other women who had admired him from afar cooed, "What a lucky woman I was to be with such a wonderful man!"

After a few weeks we started making cakes and savouries to sell at the weekends. It gave a big boost to trade. But there was precious little profit to be made. The shop was situated in a street just off the main street, and the general opinion was that if I were to find a premises in the main street, turnover would improve dramatically. Soon after this, a shop in the main street became vacant and I was assured that this was the break that I had been waiting for, and moving into the main street guaranteed that the business would thrive!

I approached the owner of the shop. His wife used the premises as a shoe shop and had decided to give it up. The rent was £25 a week more than I had been paying in the other little shop. But, hey! It was in the main street and furthermore, it had a toilet. There wasn't one in the other shop. If I needed to go, I had to lock the shop and go to the public toilet. It also had a large stock room. The other shop only had a small stock room.

My boyfriend had made a new counter for the first shop. There was quite a long old counter in this new shop and we decided to put the two of them together and have a very long counter. We varnished the floor. My boyfriend beautifully painted the shop name on to the glass window. Finally we moved the stock and put a larger order in than usual anticipating the increase in turnover. We baked on Thursday evenings, cakes and savouries to sell in the shop on Fridays, and we baked again on Fridays, cakes and savouries, plus I also did big bowls of vegetarian Indian food. People came from all over for the cooked food, but the shop, if anything, was quieter than it was on the side street.

Health food shops do seem to attract some very odd people. This second shop had a large floor space in front of the long counter. Sometimes, and more noticeably on quiet days, I would be party to some nutcase using the floor like an informal stage, and be treated to a performance of them doing a detailed breakdown of their ailments, often accompanied by much striding up and down. On a bad day, I could get several performances, in succession.

Chapter 40

A change was in the offing. I was still very asthmatic, but still loved walking. However, I struggled to get my breath if it was windy and struggled walking up hills, having to stop and rest frequently. Sometimes the inhaler made no difference, no matter how many times I used it. Sometimes, I couldn't even breath in deeply enough to make proper use of it. My doctor warned me of the dangers of over using an inhaler. He said that regular overuse could cause my lungs to collapse and I could die. So what was I supposed to do when I felt like no air was entering into my lungs and I was gasping, desperate for breath?

My boyfriend's cottage was in a most unusual position right in the middle of the main street, but he had a notion that he would like a change.

Meanwhile, I was totally baffled as to why business was poor. We had moved the business into a shop in the main street. We had worked at making the shop attractive. I spent ages, regularly changing window displays and would then sit in the quiet shop, at a loss as to what else could be done. It was during this time that I was to find that there is a right and a wrong side to be on a street. Many times, I had noticed people walking on the other side of the street, looking in the shop windows of the shops opposite. By the time they had passed the second shop it was too late for our shop to catch their eye.

I walked up the street on the same side as our shop. The shops opposite caught my eye. The front of our shop was just lightly angled back, in a way that made it invisible. People would cross the street to look at the other shops and, apart from the ones who knew it was there, it was actually possible not to notice our shop at all. I mentioned this to my boyfriend and he agreed.

Now, across the road, further up, were two shops in a very prominent position. A rather eccentric Dutch woman and her even more eccentric husband ran a craft supplies business from them. They had been trying to sell the shops and the business as a going concern for quite some time. My boyfriend happened to be doing some work for this woman in her home, making fancy covers for radiators. She had gone on, at some length, about the number of time wasters that had come to look at the properties, to which my boyfriend had apparently replied that if he had the money, he would buy them. Ever one to spot an opportunity, the woman had suggested that maybe they could come to some arrangement.

My boyfriend had been in his cottage for a good few years. It had been bought as a wreck and he, with his fathers help, had done a beautiful job of renovating it, but there were still some unfinished corners. The bathroom had never been tiled. He told me that he had never managed to come up with a suitable idea for the tiling. When I was still full of hope and optimism for the restaurant I had bought quite a lot of plain coloured tiles, intending to break them up into small pieces and make a mosaic sign to go above the front of it. Events overtook me but I still had the tiles and I asked him if he would like me to tile his bathroom with them. The colours would complement the bathroom suite which was avocado. It took me ages, but I did eventually finish it. In the deep set window recess, I added extra interest in the form of a simple mosaic of a plant in a pot. I'd finished it off by buying some antique lace and putting it in the window. He seemed pleased with the result, though, I suspected, not quite so pleased that I was getting attention for my creativity.

Anyway, he was happy to let me decorate the place, varnish the floors and make new curtains for the living room. Apart from the back yard, the property was in a saleable condition. I made a suggestion for the back yard and drew a rough sketch. He seemed a bit reluctant to tackle it, even though he quite liked the idea.

It had been agreed with the owners that we could start off by renting the other premises further up the road. The main shops were still full of all manner of craft materials, but there was a smallish room that was empty that could, at a pinch, be used as a shop temporarily. The owner and her husband, who had been a lawyer and also a High Court judge in South Africa, would work out a purchase lease, in due course.

My boyfriend's cottage was put up for sale. I suggested that we might manage to make a bit of extra money if we let it out to holiday makers whist he was waiting for a sale. So we did that and moved the shop into the tiny cramped room and we moved into the rather uncomfortable rooms above. He had told me that when his girlfriend left she had said that she did not wish to make any claim on the property, but when she became aware that it was to be sold, she did come forward, wanting her share of the proceeds. Apparently, she had made quite a big contribution and had helped with mortgage payments etc.

This was a worry as by the time he had paid off the mortgage and put a down payment on the purchase lease, there would now be no funds available whatsoever for any renovation. A new worry arrived with the purchase lease documents. I had been trying not to get involved with the business side of the purchase since I was not in a position to make any financial contribution towards it. But, reading through the very long and complex document, I was alarmed to see that the amount that he would finally end up paying for the property, was far more than the price that I was under the impression had been agreed and this had also included interest. Fear began to grip me. A feeling of "deja vu" seeped into my brain about the possible consequences of signing this document and formally entering into the arrangement, the time scale of which was 30 years. I told my boyfriend of my fears and said that I thought it would be financial suicide to continue. He, however, thought that I was just a silly woman and confirmed that he was happy with the deal. I became insistent that he visit the couple and try to get them to revise the agreement. He wagged a finger at me and suggested that I bear in mind that not yet a hundred years had passed since women had been given "the vote."

At this, I flew into a rage and went to strike him, but didn't. I just walked away into another room and put a plastic bag over my head instead. He followed me through and took it off and walked away. Our relationship had all but ended.

Chapter 41

The anticipated surge in turnover that had not happened when the business moved into the main street caused other ripples. I had not been able to contribute to the mortgage on my mothers property. She was in receipt of a reasonable income, though, and was managing to keep up with the payments. From time to time, she would go and visit my two half brothers in England. Sometime previously, she had made over to them the house that she owned there. My brother, who had worked on the restaurant project with me, said that the experience had given him the confidence together with his younger brother, to tackle a renovation project of their own and so they decided to sell their house. It sold without too much difficulty and they managed to buy a disused former village hall.

Eventually they got plans passed for conversion of this into a residential property. It was a big project. They managed it, and ended up with a very attractive home. They built an extension which provided a garage and a large extra bedroom. This was for my mother's use and the thought, with some encouragement from the boys, of going to live there permanently, had great appeal. Eventually, this was what she decided that she would do, and she put her cottage up for sale. A buyer was found and she paid off the mortgage and left the Island, to take up residence with my brothers.

Although I had never been particularly close to my mother, I was sad at her leaving. She, on the other hand seemed very happy at the prospect of this new situation.

I was now in a very unhappy situation with my boyfriend. He had taken to sitting in a different room to me, reading the Guardian newspaper, listening to classical music and existing almost entirely on cheese and onion pasties. Now, beside myself with anxiety, I suggested that this very poor diet was making him brain dead and he could not appreciate the predicament he was in danger of getting himself into. Naturally he thought I was a silly paranoid woman.

He bought himself a planer thicknesser (for the uninitiated, it is a machine for smoothing rough timber). This he took up to one of the upper rooms which he turned into a workshop and busied himself making a very artistic bathroom cabinet. This would have been fine, but for the water that poured in, unchecked, through the bathroom ceiling everytime it rained. A man who was giving up his shop further down the main street expressed an interest in buying my boyfriend's cottage. He said that he would pay the asking price if the structure at the back, which I had suggested, was installed. My 'boyfriend', grudgingly set about constructing it and the sale went through.

Now I was really scared, but for some reason our potential 'leasors' (leasers?) were in no great hurry to get him to sign the lease agreement and suggested that he put his money in the bank and let it earn some interest.

The little tiny shop was actually quite busy and I looked forward to moving into the better of the two shops that he was intending to buy. It never occurred to me that he would be incapable of resolving the misunderstanding over the price. We had, by this time, begun to use separate rooms. As usual, it was me that had migrated to another room.

Whilst all this was going on, I had a very disturbing phone call from my brother, to say that our mother had fallen off the edge of the raised garden at the back of their house, on to the terrace and had been taken to hospital with a broken leg. Very upsetting. I phoned the hospital and spoke to my mother. Initially, she seemed all right in herself, but the leg was very badly broken with both the tibia and fibia being shattered and broken away below her knee, in such a way that there was no way that the break could be pinned. I phoned every few days but a couple of weeks passed and I got the impression that she was losing the plot somewhat. I felt compelled to go over and would have gone sooner if I wasn't so broke.

I told my "boyfriend", what had happened and said that I must go over and please, would he look after the shop in my absence. He had plans of his own. Off I went. My brother met me at the Airport and that evening I was able to visit my mother. She did seem brighter for my visit. We played scrabble. I visited again the next day but had to leave on the third. Several times I had tried to phone the shop but had not managed to get a reply. I had arranged to call at Banbury whilst I was away and visit a spice wholesaler as we had talked about extending our range of Herbs and Spices. We had changed the shop name to "The Herb and Spice Shop". At the Banbury wholesalers, I picked up some of the more unusual spices and also novelty packs, to add to our range of goods. I was going back on the train and plane from Liverpool.

Sitting on the railway platform, I was visited by a sudden

fit of depression. An express train was due to pass through within the next few minutes and I briefly toyed with the idea of throwing myself under it. But even as I mused on the idea, the train flashed through and I carried on my journey, not in the best of spirits.

Arriving at Liverpool, I walked past someone selling the leaflets for "Shelter ', the homeless charity. It crossed my mind that I could be one step away from being homeless myself.

It was a relief to board the plane back to the Isle of Man. The insecure thoughts left me and I began to feel a bit more optimistic. I was looking forward to seeing my "boyfriend", I wondered if the little break might have helped and perhaps there may have been a change of perspective for both of us. He came to pick me up at the Airport, but had a very long face. Unsmiling, he put my bags in the car and drove back to Peel, not speaking whilst I made attempts at conversation. Just as we approached the outskirts he said, "Oh, by the way, I've moved out. I couldn't stay with you the way you were."

I was totally and utterly stunned. I really had not expected that. He parked the car outside the entrance to the flat above the shop, lifted my bags out, put them inside the front door and left. In a trance, I walked up to the living room and sat down. Dusty was getting old now, 16, and losing her eye sight. She needed to have drops put in her eyes twice a day and he hadn't bothered to do that so her eyes were caked and dry. I got a bowl and bathed them and put her drops in and then sat down and cried until my shock and sadness were spent.

Chapter 42

Now I knew why he hadn't been answering the phone. He was frantically moving his things out. He had told me quite early on in our relationship that he was a coward. I hadn't dwelt on the statement or it's potential. The next day was Sunday. The owner of the shop came to see me. I think that she was probably as shocked as I was. She told me that my "boyfriend" had gone to see her and told her that I wasn't sleeping with him anymore and so he was leaving. It was mid September again, four years since I fancied that I had fallen in love with him.

I asked if we could still work something out and I was able to stay where I was, for the time being. Another thing that was hard to ignore with this shop was the quite remarkable amount of coincidence that occurred. I would often place a special order with a supplier for a customer for a product that I did not normally stock. I usually got my large orders once a month, with a top-up half way through, if I was running short of anything. Then there were the small orders from different companies, supplements for instance which would come in the post. So various items could be arriving every day. The curious thing was that a customer could turn up unexpectedly, often from quite a distance away, and without first phoning to check whether or not whatever it was that they wanted had arrived, and manage to call in at the shop often within an hour of whatever it was having been delivered. They would be delighted and it would be put down to a lucky coincidence. But was it, though?

When my boyfriend left, he left behind what he didn't want, for me to deal with. I tried to phone him, but was never allowed to speak to him and had to speak to his mother. I asked what I was supposed to do with this "stuff" and was told to send it to the tip! The following Sunday, I put a small table on the pavement outside the shop and piled it up with his left behind bits, together with a notice which read,

"SURPLUS TO REQUIREMENTS. PLEASE HELP YOURSELF"

Sunday mornings in Peel are very quiet, hardly a soul about, and yet within minutes of my putting the table out on the pavement, it was emptied. I repeated this exercise several times and managed to get rid of all the small stuff.

Just lucky? I wasn't so sure.

The next day I began sorting out more bits and pieces downstairs in the shop. I had the use of a friend's car and intended closing the shop at lunchtime and taking these items to the tip. Among them was a high kitchen stool, it's seat covered in a wood grain effect vinyl. Minutes before I closed the shop for lunch, an elderly man arrived (this man had a habit of coming to the shop mid-afternoon, never in the morning or at lunchtime), he stood thoughtfully, looking at the stool, which I had placed in the shop doorway. After a few moments he mentioned that he had an identical stool at home, but that the seat was ripped. He wondered if I knew where he could get some vinyl like that on my stool to repair his. I gave him the stool and a lift home. Whatever he had come to get from the shop he forgot.

The curious thing was the timing. He did not have a car. So, if he had not arrived at the shop when he did (pretty fine timing) he would not have had his replacement stool. Another day, opening the shop after the lunchtime break, a customer arrived in the shop, quite delighted. He had just been to the "civic" looking for an electric fire. Curiously

142

enough, the one that he picked up had been dropped off by me some twenty minutes earlier. This all added to the character and interest of the shop.

So the days rolled by, I was very sad, but life had calmed down a bit. My landlady was agreeable to my moving into the more attractive of the two shops in the New Year. If the turn-over improved, there might even be the possibility of my buying it after all. She was going away to see her relatives in the Netherlands in December. I asked if she would mind if I cleared the craft items out of the shop which I was going to move into and put them into the shop which wasn't being used whilst she was away. I couldn't see the possibility of any progress otherwise. She was agreeable to that and whilst she was away, friends and customers helped me to shift her stock into the shop next door. Then I sanded the empty shop floor, gave the walls a coat of paint and moved my shop again. This was the fourth move. This shop had lovely old fashioned curved windows either side of the doorway. There was nothing across the road to attract the attention of passers by and business, at last,began to improve. The turnover slowly increasing a little each week.

My "boyfriend" was living with his mother, I would see him from time to time, passing by on the other side of the street. Understandably, the family wanted nothing to do with me now and I knew that I would have been branded as a very unpleasant woman. The grapevine was very active and I was told that his mother had put her house up for sale and that, upon it's sale, they were going to move to Scotland. He had already apparently been to view properties. They left soon after. I carried on in the shop.

It wasn't long before my landlady began to make her presence felt. She would come and hang around in the shop and hover around the customers, trying to engage them in conversation. This I found extremely irritating but was powerless to do anything about it. She also refused point blank to re-instate the partition between the two shops and would come in, almost every day to use the lavatory in the other shop but would walk through my shop to get to it. It hadn't escaped her attention that the shop was becoming busier and she began to ask on a daily basis whether I had managed to arrange anything with the bank yet. I explained that she would need to be patient a while longer, as the business needed time to stabilise in order for the bank or any other source to be confident that the income was consistent enough to secure a loan.

It didn't take long for her patience to wear thin, and mine as well for that matter, over her constant walking through the shop to use the lavatory on the other side. We had a bit of a spat. The next day, I received a note from her husband, written in his huge scrawly handwriting, informing me that the rent was to be increased. The next time she came, I tackled her over this. I had bought a lot of red lentils and weighed them up into 500 gram bags. I then made a lentil mountain the main feature of my window display. I took a packet of lentils from the display and asked if she had any idea how many of these I had to sell, in order to pay her rent. I made12p profit on a pack.

Naturally, she took exception to this and the following week the rent was raised again. A few weeks later, it was raised again. In six weeks, it almost doubled. I used to put around seventy hours a week into the shop. For this, I took50p an hour. I decided I had better get an evening job, in order to pay the rent and took a job, at a local restaurant, several nights a week.

Chapter 43

I was back to being very tired and broke and being harassed by someone who was drunk with power and once more, I was powerless to do anything about it. I would have to close the shop. She clearly wanted me out. I let her know that I was going to close and put a notice in the window, accordingly.

Then, a few weeks before I was due to close, one of the ladies from a nearby hairdresser's came to see me. She told me that they had a room at the back of their building with a side entrance and that if it would help, I could have it for my shop for £50 a week, to include rates and electricity.

I felt I had to give it a go and prepared to move the shop, this time to a side street, off the main street. From somewhere, yet again, I found some enthusiasm. I papered the walls of the new shop with a William Morris wallpaper and sent for some hops to hang around the top of the walls. It looked lovely. I moved everything. I made a little sign to fix on the street corner, pointing the way to the entrance to the shop. I put another sign on the wall outside the shop, pointing the way in. I made little cards, with a map, to show customers the new location of the shop. As usual though, I made mistakes. Another eccentric who owned the delapidated cottage next door to the shop said that I could have the use of the cottage rent free, if it would help me to keep the shop going as he felt that the shop was an asset to the town.

He then went abroad, working, and didn't leave me a key. My landlady became kinder and said I could stay in the flat over the shop a little longer. It was months before the owner of the cottage came back, and he had actually forgotten that he had offered me the use of it, for free, if it meant that I could keep the shop going. Slowly, recollection dawned and he took me to have a look at it. He informed me that the outside toilet was working. Inside, the power supply was obsolete and there was none. He fed a cable through from the property next door, which he also owned and from where he and his wife sold antiques at the week-ends. On the cable that he had run through from the adjoining property he plugged an extension socket. He had no intention of getting the property rewired.

Well, nothing else for it but to try to make some sort of comfort. The floor in the hallway had rotted and crumbled away in the middle. The sides remained, giving a slanting edge to the earth floor underneath. I really hadn't got much choice though. As usual I hoped that circumstances would improve. For the first week after moving the shop. I opened it on a part-time basis while I tried to do something with the cottage. The owner had got quite carried away, bringing all manner of useful clutter back from the tip. A rusty cooker, a kitchen table and some chairs..... Some comfort was to be gained from the fact that there were working fireplaces. I needed a coal bunker, but on checking the prices, found that I could not afford one. However, coincidence struck again, and on a Sunday, when I had planned to borrow a friend's car to go to the tip, I got what I can only describe as a "subconscious nudge" which made me feel that I should get to the tip as early as possible. There in the tip was just what I wanted, a coal bunker, just the exact size that I wanted! Now, I really did think I could draw a conclusion about coincidence. What else could it be? Other than that subconsciously we are constantly "net working" and all manner of help is at hand, it would appear that all we have to do is respond to those little subconscious "nudges", or even in some cases, warnings. Perhaps I had a subconscious warning of danger on the day of my motor accident, all I had needed was less than a minutes delay and my grandmother and I would have been spared.

Anyway, then there was some stormy weather and the roof lost a few slates. Now the rain was coming in and some of the roof timbers did not look too good. I realised that this was not going to work. My landlady said I could move back into the other flat for the time being, so I did.

In the intervening period, though, the customers who had managed to find their way to the shop, now situated in the side street had become confused by the opening hours. I quickly rectified the situation and went back to opening normal hours. However, they also seemed to have become confused by the many changes of location. It was hopeless. Trade did eventually begin to pick up but it took six months, and by the time it did, I was struggling to pay my suppliers and order new stock. Slowly I came to terms with the inevitable, I decided on a last trading day and informed my shop landlady and my customers. It was six weeks away.

Now I had to find a job. I scanned the situations vacant in the local papers. I ran through imaginary interviews in my head, where the interviewer would ask me about my qualifications, and then comment that I didn't appear to have stuck at anything. The other comment that I had had sometimes in the past was that in view of all the experience I had, I was over qualified. Pretty hopeless. Although I had done lots of different things I hadn't actually got any qualifications and on top of that, my clothes were shabby.

What on earth was I going to do ....

What was uppermost in my mind was that, whatever I did, there must be no premises, no partner and no staff. Eventually, I thought of what I could do and made a list. I decided that I would become a Girl Friday. I drew a picture of the head and shoulders of what I hoped looked like a friendly, helpful person, holding a mop, a hammer, a screw driver, and a paintbrush. At the top I made the suggestion that help was at hand in the form of "Friday". Next to the picture I wrote my list of the services that I could offer ...

Staff cover (holidays and sickness)
Basic typing
Decorating
Cleaning
Gardening
Picture hanging
Curtain making
Shopping
Ironing
Cooking (vegetarian and special diets)
Etc etc.

HAVE YOU A PROBLEM?

FRIDAY IS AT HAND WITH MANY USEFUL SPECIALIST SKILLS:

From: Filling in to cover staff shortages, e.g. experienced waitress, sales assistant

To: Basic typing, decorating, cleaning, gardening, picture hanging, curtain making, vegetarian cooking & cooking for special diets, shopping, ironing etc. etc.

Please telephone for rates / quotes.

Rates start at £5.00 for ½ hour - reducing for multiples of hours worked.

I put my mobile phone number on and invited people to telephone. I took this drawing, and list to the toy shop which also provided a photocopying service and asked them to print 50 copies for me. I figured that the counter in the dry cleaners might be a good place to leave some of these flyers. The idea being that if people could afford regular dry cleaning, they might also be in need of other help. The people that ran the dry cleaners were kind and had no objection to my leaving some of my leaflets on their counter. I also handed out leaflets to my customers and busied myself winding the shop down. A familiar experience came with my last day in the shop. I had actually managed to sell everything right down to the dried hops that I had hung around the top of the walls. My plan was to keep £250 back, in cash. This was to tide me over, for a while, until I could see whether or not my new idea was going to work.

I didn't make quite enough to pay all the money off that I owed to my suppliers and was left with a small amount outstanding to one of them, which they agreed to let me pay off in instalments, as and when I could.

I also had some useful dried foods left (that I could make meals with), which would also help the budget. I wondered what would happen. On the third day of my wait, I got a phone call from a lady who had been a regular customer in the shop. She wondered if I would be interested in doing some cleaning for her. Interested! I was so relieved.

That was my first customer in my new venture and she needed five hours cleaning help every week. Her phone call was the one that gave me hope. The next day, I got a phone call from an elderly lady who needed help in her garden. Whilst I was working in her garden, her neighbour called to me and asked if I would go and do her garden. Then I got a call from another person who needed cleaning help. It looked like I might just manage to make a small living.

Chapter 44

When my boyfriend had left, I was lost, I had no-one to wander around the shops with, or go walking. In that sad state, I met someone else. He was temporarily living with his sister. He was very kind and I think we were both in need of some company, though he didn't want to go for walks in the country or spend an afternoon wandering around the shops. I mused on the saying "Better to have loved and lost, than never to have loved at all", I had had quite a romantic time for a while.

My new friend had recently inherited some money and property, a potential tiny building plot and an old car. The old car he gave to me. This was great as it meant that I could go further afield, now, to work. He decided that he would build a tiny cottage on his tiny building plot, and I would have first choice of renting it, if I wished. Once again, it looked as though I would emerge from a crisis, but there seemed to have been so many. On the other hand, with each new crisis, I picked up a new skill. I decided that bad luck might actually be good for a person. I had become a survivor. I was far more awake and aware, now, than I had ever been. Experience had changed my perspective on life and I gladly took whatever work came my way.

Plans were put in for the tiny building plot and with minor alterations here and there they were subsequently passed. Work began on the tiny dwelling. My friend had a big financial commitment to his wife, despite the parting, and the building would be done on a very tight budget, rather than leave his family short of money, which was only right and proper, running very low on funds, right at the end, when Douglas came to the rescue, yet again.

He was now living in Ramsey and working as an apprentice carpet and flooring fitter. He was sharing a rented cottage with one of his friends whose marriage had broken up. From time to time, they would have some other relationship refugee camping out with them. There was nearly always someone who was temporarily homeless, sleeping on the sofa. Douglas seemed to have a natural talent for the flooring work and was quickly becoming skilled. He was sent on training courses,to learn the more complicated aspects of fitting. Like me, each new crisis was also bringing him a new skill. Money had run out by the time it came to screeding the floor at the little cottage. Douglas came and, together, we put the screed down, which would make the rough concrete floor smooth enough, to lay either tiles or carpet on. I decided that I would prefer to have the floor tiled and Douglas was able, through the company that he was working for, to provide me with tiles at trade price, and then fit them for love. How lucky was I! I provided the shower surround. My friend managed to get the tiling done and by April, it was ready to move into. It was tiny, only about 9 feet wide and consisted of three rooms, in a row, with a tiny hall, separating the bedroom from the living room and kitchen. The back half of the hall formed the bathroom.

Once again I set about trying to make myself comfortable. There was a narrow strip of ground at the front where I could grow some flowers. There was even an area where

I could park the car. The rent was to be £50 a week. I had somewhere to live and I now had a reasonably reliable income from a few regular customers, plus extra money, from time to time, from other oddments of work. Some income now was coming from my former landlady. She had decided to sell off the craft stock that she still had, piled up in her shop and also, on the first floor rooms above. I helped her to bring stock into what had been my shop, and on Saturdays we worked at selling it off. Business was brisk, with people crowding in to grab the best of the bargains.

She also decided that she could use some help in her house. Fortunately I had had experience of her house whilst I still had the shop and knew what to expect. She had approached me, whilst I had still been living with my artist boyfriend, in his cottage, with regard to my cooking an Indian banquet for her husbands 75th birthday. His daughter, from his first marriage and her son were coming over for the occasion. We worked out a menu and I arranged to do this meal for them on a Sunday. Someone who was a regular customer in the shop, on having heard that I was to do the meal, came into the shop one day and handed me a paper bag, saying "I think you might need these,"I looked in the bag, and took out a surgical glove that would reach over my elbow and a face mask. She said no more and I found the gesture highly amusing.

The day before the dinner, my boyfriend manned the shop in the afternoon, whilst I shopped for what I needed for the dinner party. Most of the next day had been taken up with doing basic preparations. I pre-cooked the meat for the curries, the rice, and the starters and the desserts. The curries I would complete in situ, adding extra traditional spices to give them their authentic flavour.

By 4p.m, I was ready. Everything was packed up in a couple of boxes. There were naan breads, popadoms which I would cook at the house, pickles, chutneys, the pre-prepared meats, gravies, pilau rice, salad etc. With the gap in activity, I had a moment, a twinge of apprehension, and my mind went back to the surgical glove and the face mask. I took a couple of aspirin. To add to my suspicion, my boyfriend, who had at first been going to come and help me, now decided that he wouldn't. But he would drive me round and come and pick me up when I was ready. I'd worked under enormous pressure in the past. I would manage.

So we arrived and I rang the doorbell. I heard much unlocking of doors. First the door leading from the kitchen to the back door porch. Once through this, she relocked it before unlocking the outer door. The two boxes were taken from the car and placed in this porch and the outer door was re-locked. I watched my boyfriend make his getaway. Now she unlocked the kitchen door, the porch smelt bad, but the stench emitting from the kitchen and the house itself was unbelievable. So was the kitchen. I walked into the middle of it, holding the first of my two boxes and surveyed filthy worktops, piled high with debris, the draining board piled up with dirty dishes, the sink, full of dirty water and more dishes, the filthy cupboard fronts, the filthy floor, so dirty it was not possible to distinguish the actual colour. This had a perimeter of discarded empty bottles, empty packets and hair. Five cats and a collie dog lived in the house and never set foot out of it. It was beyond revolting.

"Are you alright June?" She was watching me from the doorway.

My first instinct was to turn and leave, but she had paid for all the prepared food in the boxes and also my fee and I did need the money. A moments pause,

"I need somewhere to put this down," I said, indicating the box.

She put her arm across the depth of the worktop, and slid, the assortment of clutter along the grease and hair that coated it, into a more compact arrangement in the corner. I put my box on it. She made room for the other box, on top of a redundant twin tub washing machine, by taking the cat food bowls off it.

"I can manage now," I said "I'll have to make a bit of space first, if you don't mind.!"

That was alright. I was introduced to the daughter and her son who seemed completely unfazed by their surroundings.

I had used my inhaler before I came out. I quickly set about sorting out the things in the sink. There wasn't a plug in it. It was just blocked and, judging from the smell, the stuff had been sitting in it for several days. Having cleared the plug hole, I then poured boiling water in, to try to dissolve the blockage. I had to ask to be let out of the kitchen, to check the drain outside. We followed the same routine as before, first the kitchen door was unlocked, then relocked, once we were in the porch. Then the outside door was unlocked. She waited in the porch whilst I cleared the blocked drain and then let me back in. And the same performance was repeated to get back into the kitchen.

I could now make space. There was a dishwasher full of washed dishes. I emptied that and rinsed some of the pile on and around the sink and loaded it up again. Now I could start cooking, almost an hour after I had arrived. I was starting to get wheezy. I used my inhaler and slipped up a gear. Not so funny now, the long glove and surgical mask. The top of the oven was in the same condition as every other surface in the kitchen. The inside of the oven was as I expected it to be.

I heated oil and cooked the popadoms and served them with a variety of chutneys,pickles and dips. While they were eating those, I heated the starters I had already made, samosas, pakora, and onion bagees. I quickly got those out. I was starting to wheeze again, I was starting to really struggle breathing. On with the curries. This final preparation would take roughly half an hour. I had the naan breads warming in the oven. By now I was having to bend over against the work top, periodically, as I struggled to breath. Now the inhaler was having no effect whatsoever. I couldn't take a deep enough breath to use it. By some miracle, I managed to serve their meal. They loved it. They were happy and I could phone my boyfriend to come and get me. So having had the cooking experience, future visits to her home did not shock me. I bought face masks and wore them so that I would not be breathing in the rotten dusty air. I would shower, change my clothes and wash my hair when I got home and found that, this way, I could survive it.

Chapter 45

I was quite well settled into my little cottage now. I had a bit more space in my mind to think and I was becoming obsessed with coincidences. I was so aware of them now. One of my friends husbands suggested I write about my observations. I did. And someone else that I knew suggested that I send my article to a quite eminent psychiatrist. I did.

He clearly thought that I was nuts and sent me a reply, asking if I was unwell and suggested that I see my doctor.

This was embarrassing. But, I had gone off the rails once before and I began to wonder if the relentless adversity was taking it's toll on me. There was just one thing that I could change. I was still on a vegetarian diet, although I did take supplements in the form of B vitamins,to make up for the nutritional deficiency of the vegetarian diet. I thought about the customers who came into the shop who were vegetarians, and on the whole, if they weren't crackers they were not in the best of health. I thought about Adolph Hitler who was a vegetarian, and his distorted vision and the resultant holocaust.

Stephen King-Hall in his book '*Our own Times 1913-1938*' describes the reality of the Great War of 1914–1918 as more astonishing than any work of fiction. And that it can claim to be the most remarkable single activity ever undertaken by man. It was more unique and defied every precedent in every way. It was more horrible, more heroic, more gigantic, more nearly universal, more costly, more destructive, more catastrophic, more highly organised, more chaotic, more everything, more nothing, more significant,more meaningless, than anything that had happened before,in human history.

Having given more thought to this, I thought, perhaps it isn't enough to supplement a diet with supplements. I really didn't ever want to go nuts again and so I re-introduced meat back into my diet. Not easy at first as I had developed quite an aversion to it. But I persevered and I did begin to feel, mentally, more focused.

I doubt if I would ever have found a job which would have brought me into contact with such a wide and sometimes alarming look at life. I was drawn more and more to gardening work which almost proved to be my downfall. I was still doing cleaning work and still had the woman who had become my first customer and a couple of small, but regular, cleaning jobs besides. This just about covered the rent and living. The rest of my income was made up almost entirely from gardening work.

November came, and with it, a rainy spell, it rained almost constantly for six weeks. I would watch the flood water surging down the road, day after day. I resolved to take on more cleaning work. Another year dawned, this relationship hadn't progressed at all. I could see that it was not going to progress. My friend seemed happy to have me as a sort of low maintenance mistress, and I was giving quite considerable thought to the fact that I wasn't sure that I even liked intimacy, or had even ever liked it that much. I fretted over this for a while and eventually decided that I must say something about it. My friend was now living in a flat of his own in Douglas and his life was much more settled. I anxiously broached the subject, I need not have worried, as he was perfectly understanding, we ended our involvement on friendly terms and I stayed in the cottage.

This turned out to be provident, as not many months after this, Douglas found himself in a position where he was going to need to find somewhere else to live. His landlord had made the property over to his son-in-law who now wanted to renovate it and then sell. Douglas and his friend had been given notice to leave. I said to Douglas that if the worst came to the worst he could camp out in the cottage for a while. As it happened, things turned out that way and he came to stay. I suggested that he have the bedroom and I would sleep on the sofa, this, because I still had Dusty, now nearly eighteen. I also had three cats. The three cats had come about via the Dutch woman. She had an adorable little pewter grey, tabby cat. Then she acquired a ginger tom kitten, but before she got around to having the tom neutered, he did the business with the tabby. I suspected that the kittens that she produced might be very attractive and had asked if I might have one, thinking that she wouldn't want to keep them all.

Two kittens were born, one was a tabby with very lovely markings, the other was a small nondescript looking little thing, mostly charcoal in colour with a small flash of ginger on one flank. This one I chose. It seemed a safe choice, as I knew the Dutch woman to be prone to jealousies. Eight weeks later, I took my kitten home. It was a female and I called her Minerva. Rather unfortunately, she grew into a beautiful cat with a long coat and brindle stripes and was much coveted by her mother's owner. I kept her in when she was on heat, but there's always the one time, and she got out. It was while I was still living in the shop building that I had hoped to buy and she had got out of a second floor window which had only been open about an inch. I had searched and searched for her to no avail. Two weeks later, she came back and some time after that it was clear that she was pregnant. I let the pregnancy run on.

On July 4th there was much scrabbling about and I found her tearing up newspaper and making a makeshift nest. The same day, she produced one little black kitten. It was a relief that there was only one. I decided that I would keep it. It would have a kind home with me. Minerva was very restless though and couldn't seem to settle, constantly changing her position. I wasn't quite sure what to do. She didn't actually seem unwell or in any pain and was a lovely mother to her kitten. Two weeks later, she produced two more kittens, twice as big as the first one. Another black one and a ginger. I decided to keep the two black ones and let the ginger one go. It went to the lady who had given me the surgical glove and face mask. The Dutch woman had been incandescent with rage, and claimed, that the woman to whom I had given the kitten was not fit to keep animals. She did, in fact, run a shelter for injured hedgehogs and could have up to thirty in her care. She was a very caring person. Why does life have to be so complicated? Anyway that's how I ended up with three cats. The female was subsequently spayed and the toms neutered. And that's why I slept on the couch and let Douglas have the bedroom. He didn't feel quite the same about animals as I did. Besides he did have a problem with allergies with them. I did as well, but the inhaler helped and also antihistamines.

Chapter 46

A couple of months passed and Douglas still hadn't found any alternative accommodation. It was while we were living in these cramped conditions, that one day, when I happened to be working in a nearby garden, I chanced to be within earshot of an open conservatory window and overheard a snippet of conversation pass between my customer and her daughter. The other daughter and her husband had been renting a fairly large house whilst they awaited completion on a new house that they planned to move into. They would be vacating it in about a month's time. I downed tools and knocked on the conservatory door, explaining that I had just caught the bit of conversation concerning the sister about to be moving out of a rented house. They filled me in on it's location and gave me the landlord's phone number. It turned out be an old house that I had always admired. Another coincidence, and I was fascinated by coincidence.

When Douglas got back that evening, I mentioned that I had heard of a larger property, nearby, that was soon to be available. We took a walk up the road and I showed him where it was. It had a walled garden and a garage, we decided that I should get in touch with the landlord and explore the possibility of renting it. Some days later, I met up with the landlord. The property was a bit run down and the rent was just about affordable. We decided to move there. There were four bedrooms plus a large attic. Someone that I knew, who wasn't too happy with her accommodation, came to stay with us as well, which made the rent and bills more manageable.

As far as relationships were concerned, Douglas seemed to be following in my footsteps, and been involved in a stormy on and off relationship with the mother of his daughters for about ten years. Before coming to stay with me, he did ask her if she wanted to give it one more try. She didn't, and he seemed to be pretty much "off" women. His two daughters though, my grandchildren, were a joy, and could now come and spend weekends with us at the big house. I hadn't really been able to see them as often as I would have liked, up until this point, and the next few years were to be among some of the happiest that I had experienced.

The house had two sitting rooms, one of which opened out into a conservatory. I bagged this one. Douglas and my friend bagged the two larger bedrooms, which left me with a smaller one. The other small one had bunk beds in and this became the girls' room for their visits. The attic had a narrow staircase leading up to it and was carpeted and I really liked the idea of having it for my bedroom. When we moved into the house, it was apparent that it had been used as a dumping ground and the whole of the floor was covered with a layer of black bags, discarded clothing, shoes, boots, bits of furniture, an old pushchair, discarded toys etc. The walls had been painted orange and then sponged with burgundy.

There was loads of space under the eaves and also some walk in storage space so I bagged everything up and packed it away. Then I painted the whole area white. A lot of the carpets in the house were very much the worse for wear and Douglas replaced the ones in the girls' room and the two large bedrooms. I took the carpet up in the small bedroom and sanded and stained and varnished the floorboards. It became a guest room. Douglas put new laminate flooring down in his sitting room and I took up the carpet in mine and sanded and stained and varnished the floorboards. Having the two sitting rooms worked, as we both had our own space and yet there was company if we needed it. Everyone enjoyed the conservatory. I loved having the attic as my bedroom. It was peaceful up there. If the others came in late, I wasn't disturbed. It had a velux window in the roof and was lovely and bright in the daytime. At night, I would watch the moon drift over.

I worked at my little business. When I had started it up, I had no idea what I should charge and started off at £7.50 per hour. I learnt pretty quickly that it wasn't going to be enough, though I had also born in mind that if I charged too much I wouldn't get any work. The one thing in my favour was that I was reasonably well known and trusted. When the old car that I had been given finally gave up the ghost and had to be scrapped, I applied for a credit card and bought a second hand car, a lawnmower and some useful gardening tools. I raised my hourly rate to £10 only to find that I was still running at a loss, I had to keep taking money from the credit card to meet my share of the rent and bills.

It was so easy to get credit, I could have had as many credit cards as I wanted. I took another one offering 0% interest for six months and transferred the balance to that from the first one, fully intending to get it paid off. I increased my hourly rate to £12.50 for gardening. For cleaning I kept it at £10. In no time, I found that the balance on the new card was approaching it's limit, though I was getting near to breaking even with my income. Juggling my income became a nightmare. The second car was about to gasp it's last and would have to be scrapped, as it needed costly repairs that weren't worth doing. I was turned down for a bank loan to pay off my cards (debts still being discharged to the Coroner), and get another second hand car. However I did manage to get lucky with another company offering loans and managed to get a loan for £7,500 plus interest at 10.9% making a total of £9,655.80, plus loan protection £2,066.40, making a total of £11,722.60, to be repaid over five years. I felt I had no choice but to take it. It took a matter of minutes to arrange. This loan wasn't enough to pay off all my credit cards, but at least I could go and get another car.

I took two days to search the Island for a car that I could afford. It had to be an estate car, so that I could get my tools in the back of it. I had almost given up hope when I came across a Citroen ZX in a garage in the south of the Island. I could just about afford it. There was no guarantee but I wasn't in a position to be choosy. I had to get back to work as soon as possible.

Chapter 47

It was Douglas's suggestion that we put our names down for one of the local commissioners' houses, something that would never have occurred to me, as I had always thought that I would manage to get back on my feet and manage to buy another property. I had begun to think that we would be living in this same house for ever. There didn't seem to be any sign of Douglas having any interest in having a relationship.

My health wasn't too good though, I was now using three different inhalers every day and I struggled with some of the heavier work. I couldn't manage to walk up the hill, from the bottom of the town, to where we now lived, without having to make several stops for my breathing to settle down, enough for me to carry on. At night I would wake up, struggling to breathe, and then struggle to use an inhaler, and still have precious little relief from it. I had also got problems with my legs filling with fluid again, accompanied by unbearable itching which was always worse at night. And then there was the spot. It had arrived around my 50th birthday at the corner of my mouth, and I had done what most people would do. I squeezed it. But, it didn't behave in a normal way, it didn't discharge it's contents and then heal. Instead it got angry and bigger. It would itch, unbearably. I tried every natural remedy I could find to try to deal with it. It didn't seem to be infected so I treated it as a wart, and then as a fungal problem. It resisted vigorously and began to spread. It would granulate but never healed. If I touched it, it would bleed. If I didn't touch it, it would itch unbearably and then I would touch it, if only to press on it to stop the itching, The surface would sometimes begin to lift but if I touched it, again it bled. I must have tried every over the counter remedy available, for cold sores, warts, fungal problems. In desperation I went to the doctor. He scrutinised it though a magnifying glass and decided that I should use an anti-biotic stick on it. The doctor told me that it might take a long time before any effect was noticed.

I wasn't too keen on this approach, but out of desperation I tried it. It became so painful when I applied the anti-biotic stick that I gave it up, besides which, it seemed to get angrier than ever. I took to cutting out little circles of elastoplast and sticking the tiniest bit of lint in the centre of them and this I would stick over the what could only be described as sores, sores that weren't healing. Now, at both sides of my mouth. I felt like I would like to wear a box over my head when I ventured out. Douglas was convinced that it was something to do with the cleaning fluids that I used when working in people's houses. But I said it couldn't be, as I always wore gloves. I was beginning to be suspicious, though,of something that had happened some years before and was beginning to wonder if there might be a connection.

I should enlarge on this. The connection that I had begun to be suspicious about relates back to the time after I lost the restaurant. I was having endless problems with my teeth due to abscesses. I had to take a dose of Amoxicillin before each visit to the dentist, and for some time I was going to the dentist every week. Amoxicillin, as we know, kills off everything including the healthy bacteria in our gut, giving unrestricted opportunity for the intestinal fungi to spread, unchecked, through-out the body, spreading not unlike a dry rot fungus, until it becomes visible externally, e.g. toenails. I suspected the sores on my face (and I also had itchy sores on my legs), might have a connection with my taking many large doses of Amoxicillin, several years previously. I wondered if in my case it could have taken several years for the intestinal fungi to spread through my body, before appearing externally. I also wondered if, unwittingly, I had helped to proliferate the intestinal fungi, feeding it with what it would thrive on, namely, simple starches and sugars, derived from simple carbohydrates and fruit sugars, all of which were consumed in ample quantities on my vegetarian diet.

At the time, that, I was taking the Amoxicillin, I did what I thought would compensate, by eating live yogurt and taking supplements of live bacteria, promoted to introduce the "good" bacteria back into the gut. Now I was beginning to have doubts. What if the intestinal fungi had got so out of control on my vegetarian diet that, whatever I might have done at to restore balance, might have been as much use as trying to put out a raging fire by spitting on it? And what if, the delicate balance of our bodies can be dangerously upset by such aggressive treatment, and that balance may not so easily be restored and "fixed" as one might with a piece of man-made machinery?

In the meantime I wheezed around my gardening and cleaning jobs, and any other work that came my way. I felt weary and often depressed. Some of my gardening customers dealt with their garden waste themselves. Others, who were

165

not in a position to do so would rely on me to dispose of it for them. I took it to the local recycling centre. This was one of the perks of my job, as I would be able to have a look around in the covered areas, where people had dropped off stuff that they no longer needed. I had been lucky enough to pick up an almost new strimmer on one of my visits. So there I was, one day in the summer having dropped off a load of grass, having my usual poke around. A lot of books had been dropped off, boxes and boxes of them. I began to sift through them. Then one in particular caught my eye, someone had placed it on the music stand of an organ. It was entitled J.I. Rodale's *Health Treasury*. I settled for that and got back in my car and went home. At home I put J. I. Rodale's *Health Treasury* in a cupboard and forgot about it. Summer drew to an end. Autumn arrived, I had managed to raise my hourly rate to £15 an hour for gardening and £12.50 for cleaning. Even without the borrowing it would have been difficult to make ends meet petrol to buy, tools to replace, rent to pay, income tax and stamps....

On a rainy day in November when I was at home, I remembered J. I. Rodale's *Health Treasury*. I got it out of the cupboard and sat in the rocking chair in the kitchen and began to browse through it. After a little while I came across a short section on asthma. Apparently, Hippocrates, who had lived in the 5th century B.C advised that asthmatics should be wary of situations that could make them feel angry, as extreme emotion increased the severity of an attack. I could relate to that, as it had been suggested to me by my doctor, when I was experiencing health problems during my first marriage. That the fact that was that my marriage was unhappy and my poor health stemmed from this. My health was also chronically poor whenever I stayed with my mother. In this book, there was the idea that children who had been rejected by their mothers would subsequently suffer with asthma. Apparently, a test conducted on children gave results that showed 98.4 % of them felt rejected in some way either consciously or unconsciously,with or without just reason. My health had also become very poor when I lived with my artist boyfriend, and I had, at the time, put it down to the stress of living with him. No other possible cause had ever been suggested to me.

Chapter 48

I was about to be introduced to a theory which was to change my life beyond recognition for ever. There was quite a mass of information in this short section of the book, leading up to the possibility that the primary cause of asthma was, in fact, low blood sugar, which is directly linked to diet, and also correctable by diet.

At first reading, I confess that I thought this possibility highly unlikely. If, what the book suggested was true, why would I and many people like me, have been subjected to a lifetime of suffering through needless poor health?

There was a diet to follow in the book which claimed to prevent or cure low blood sugar. I decided to follow it, if only to prove that it was in fact nonsense! I copied out the diet on a couple of little pieces of card, and put one on the notice board in the kitchen and the other in my bag. This, so I had a handy reference at hand to remind me, what I should not be eating, what I should be eating, and when. In a matter of days, my asthma attacks had stopped. It was as though somebody had waved a magic wand! I did not need my inhaler, though I kept it with me. There was the underlying insecurity that an asthma attack might ambush me, unawares. But it didn't happen. After a few weeks, I went to see my Doctor. I felt quite excited and was looking forward to telling him my good news. I waited, patiently, in the waiting room for my turn. Finally, I was buzzed to go through. My Doctor was a young man, always immaculate and smiley. He asked what he could do for me, and I told him about the book that I had found in the tip, and the asthma diet. His reaction shocked me. He actually wagged a finger at me and said,

"You must take your medication every day June,"

He wrote me out a prescription for an inhaler, and I did redeem it. Just in case. I had felt bewildered by the doctor's reaction. It shook my confidence, but not for long. I persevered with the diet. I can still remember the first day I strode home up the hill from the shops in the town, breathing deeply and walking upright and feeling stronger. It was a wonderful feeling. No-one was going to take this away from me. The depression, that used to wrap around me like a fog, also went. I became more focused.

Some months later, I went back to see my doctor again. I told him that the diet was still working. He turned to his papers on his desk and said, "Oh, well, if it works for you June."

Through J. I. Rodale's book, I had become aware of research undertaken by a Dr Abrahamson. In the section on asthma, the reader is encouraged to obtain and study a book written by Dr E. M. Abrahamson. M. D. and A.W. Pezet. entitled '*Body, Mind and Sugar*'. It was out of print, so I put a request in, with a book search company, to find a copy for me. It was several weeks later that the book search company got in touch to let me know that they had located a few copies of the book, 'Body Mind and Sugar'. I requested the cheapest one and sent off my payment.

Study was becoming my preferred companion, I had done a lot of reading in the healthfood shop, in order to be able to help people to choose gluten free alternatives and dairy free alternatives, and to be able to suggest simple remedies. As a gardener, although I'd always gardened, I spent hours studying methods of pruning, planting, hedge cutting, and the needs of plants to thrive. I hadn't been to horticultural college but I had gardened, and been around gardeners all my life and already had a good general knowledge.

My book arrived. By this time, I would have happily not gone to work, in order to spend time reading it. The more I read, the more bewildered I became, and possibly shocked as well. Moreover, this book had been first published in 1951. On top of that, Dr Abrahamson acknowledges research done by other doctors, going as far back as 1869! This information deeply affected me. It pointed to the fact that I need not have had to live with my lifetime of poor health.

All the while, my health was improving but I still had a nagging insecurity, and still had an inhaler in my possession, although I had not needed to use it. While I was absorbed in all this, Douglas had started dating again, girls started to appear on the scene, and occasionally, at the breakfast table. My friend that was lodging with us, seemed to be searching for an ideal mate and went out with various desperate characters. Romance was definitely not going to blossom between her and Douglas, though they were of a similar age, she being a bit younger. They seemed to get on each other's nerves.

Then, one night, she went out and came back smitten. She wasn't sure, but she thought that she had met the man that she was looking for. Their romance blossomed very quickly. A couple of months later she went to live with him. It was a happy ever after. I was happy for her. We decided not to sub-let her room as there had been tensions from time to time and hoped that we would be able to manage the rent between us. Eventually, a new girl appeared in the house. She was different to all the rest and had an air of quiet intelligence about her. I liked her immediately. She seemed very smitten with Douglas, whereas he almost seemed slightly indifferent. The girls did chase after him and he didn't have to make a lot of effort.

Our second Christmas in this house was approaching. Another girl was persistently hanging around him, and at Christmas time things came to a head and Julie called time on the relationship. I was sad to see her go but it was none of my business. The other girl carried on hanging around, though Douglas didn't seem particularly interested in her either. Also around this time he had a worry in that he was producing an unusual amount of saliva, and had been to see the doctor and been referred to see a consultant at the hospital. He was found to have a tumour on the salivary gland, in the right hand side of his neck, which needed operating on. He was told that there was a possibility that the operation could leave him with the right hand side of his face dropped, as a result of cutting nerves. The worst case scenario was that the whole of his face could drop.

An operation was scheduled to remove the tumour and this would be sometime in the following year. Spring came and Douglas went to the hospital for a final consultation. He was seen by a foreign Registrar who seemed to be immersed in his notes, muttering something about a left breast. Douglas, unnerved by this, drew attention to the fact that it was the tumour in his neck that was to be operated on. He came home, very nervy, and became so ill in the night that he was unable to go to the hospital for his operation the next day. It was cancelled. When he went back to the hospital, he was relieved to see the Surgeon who was to perform the operation, who was able to allay his fears.

The operation was looming again. He told me that he felt lonely and thought he might phone Julie. He phoned and told her about the impending operation and what the possible outcome might be. She told him that she would love him, even if the whole of his face dropped, and so their friendship was rekindled. Julie was around most weekends and the house would be filled with her laughter. She had a little girl of five who we were also slowly getting to know. I was happy for them, and I was happy that Julie was around again. I had missed her.

I had been without asthma for over a year now and had not used an inhaler in that time. My commitment to my diet became the family joke. My friends accused me of being a bore with it. I didn't care, my life was changed. I decided to go and see my doctor again and see if his reaction would still be the same. I had a new doctor. I had to fill him in with my experience of finding the book in the tip, and my subsequent experience of really good health for the first time in my life, as a result of following the dietary recommendations given by Dr Abrahamson. This Doctor had heard of Dr Abrahamson. He was much easier to talk to than my other doctor, but he didn't seem convinced that I was not experiencing any asthma attacks, and prescribed me an inhaler. He told me that there are many different causes of asthma, and said that stress could trigger an attack. I was very disappointed but did not allow his lack of interest to dishearten me. Quite the reverse, in fact. I had now begun to revise and test Dr Abrahamsons theories on myself. I was the best guinea pig I could have had, as I had had so many health problems and I could monitor the results 24 hours a day,7 days a week,365 days a year. I resolved that I would write my own very simple and easy to follow guide on controlling asthma by diet alone.

Chapter 49

Douglas was very lucky. He had his operation and with no ill effects. His girlfriend still loved him and was now very keen that they should set up home together. He told her that if she could find a place in the country that they could afford, that he would consider it. It did sound harsh. Maybe it boiled down to "once bitten" etc. But Julie was smart and clever and found somewhere ideal remarkably quickly. He didn't move straight away. Maybe he was surprised at the new reality that now confronted him.

A few weeks passed, and any doubts there may have been in his mind went, and his departure was imminent. I had the dilemma of finding someone to share the house with me. I tried advertising the two rooms, but I think that I knew in the back of my mind that it would be very difficult to find a person or persons who didn't offend me. There were no replies to my adverts, I tried writing to some of the larger offices that may have had staff working here on short term contracts, and who might have preferred to live in a private house rather than be put up in a hotel. Again, I had no replies.

Douglas was starting to panic. He was still paying his share of the rent. I knew that I would have to find somewhere else to live. Sadness overwhelmed me, but not depression or despair as might have been the case before my change of diet. I missed Douglas, I missed my grandchildren and I missed Julie and her little girl. Every night I would go to bed and break my heart over this new situation. I put an advert in the paper,advertising for modest accommodation where I could take my cats. Dusty had died before we had left the little cottage. She was almost nineteen.

This time, I got replies to my advert. I was inundated with offers of accommodation, I guessed that was why I had had no replies to my advert. There seemed to be a surplus available. The accommodation I was offered was all way over my budget. The cats were a drawback to my taking a room in a shared house, but I had no intention of parting with them. Then, when I was about to give up hope, I got a phone call from a woman who said that she lived in a converted chapel at Derbyhaven, and it might not be what I had in mind but the upper floor was a self-contained flat which she would consider letting me have for £50 a week, plus a contribution towards the bills. I went to see her. Somehow she had worked out that I was in a fix. I brought her over to the house that I was still living in, and showed her around so that she could see that I had kept the place in good order. I couldn't move into the chapel straight away as it was crammed with stuff, so I went to stay, temporarily, with a friend who lived nearby and who had an empty garage where I could put the small amount of furniture that I had.

I then spent time at the chapel, sorting out the upstairs. My new landlady had been living in the top floor, but had had a fall, breaking both her ankles, and had moved into the flat downstairs. I worked hard at sorting out the muddle. There were already two bedroom suites in the bedroom that I was going to use and I had an antique chest of drawers that I didn't want to part with, so that had to go in there as well. I got myself organised and there was nothing stopping me moving, other than a vague feeling of unease. I wasn't quite sure about this new situation and yet I couldn't understand why. Finally, in November, I made my mind up and made the move. My new landlady had bought a second hand television for the living room, and had been watering my collection of house plants. What was I worried about? The friend that I had stayed with, temporarily, was upset at my going and my landlady had begun to wonder if I would ever move in. Life is never straight forward.

So I was there in my new place. It was actually quite pleasant, apart from the fact that my landlady chainsmoked, and the smoke drifted upstairs at the edges of the rooms, and everything reeked of smoke. I smelt like a smoker, all my clothes smelt of smoke, but it didn't trigger an asthma attack.

My landlady had two miniature chihuahua dogs. They stayed inside with just necessary visits outside for toilet needs. I had to keep the cats in, anyway, while they got accustomed to their new surroundings, but because of the dogs, they were not going to be able to go in and out through the shared front door. I took some extra evening work in a petrol station to make sure I would have my rent money each week. I gave my landlady an £25 a week toward the bills. I kept her garden area tidy. If I cooked a meal, I frequently made enough for the two of us. Since she didn't drive and the buses were pretty infrequent, if I wasn't working, but going out in the car, I usually asked her if she would like to come along. She always came.

Three weeks passed, and I opened the dormer window in the sitting room, I thought cats being cats, that mine would venture out and down the roof, onto the porch roof and into the garden below. They didn't. Instead they sat on the window sill and just looked out. January came. I had decided that things could be far worse. I was getting used to the situation and had assumed that my landlady was, as well. The fact that there was no door on the shower didn't matter, I was just very careful using it, so that the bathroom floor didn't get awash. The one time I tried to open the kitchen window, it plummeted out of sight and was just prevented from crashing down on the concrete path below by a thin leather strap that someone had used to secure it to the frame. I hadn't even begun to think about decorating the place, partly because I was broke and partly because I was still getting my bearings.

There was a phone in the living room which rang when my landlady's phone rang downstairs. She had told me that I was welcome to use the phone. I had thanked her and declined saying that I was happy enough just using my mobile. And so it happened that the second Sunday in January, I was cleaning my rooms upstairs, and was vacuuming in the living room, when her phone rang. I carried on vacuuming. There was a bureau in this room that she said that she would like to have downstairs. I finished what I was doing and went and knocked on the door of her sitting room. She was standing up, having just finished her phone call. I mentioned the bureau and noticed a sudden change in her demeanour. In a second, her face became very flushed, and then she began to shout. Why hadn't I turned the vacuum cleaner off when I heard the phone ring? I said that I didn't know that I was supposed to. Her colour was deepening by the second.

"You are so fucking selfish," she screamed, "you are a big fucking disappointment, I want you out, you can have a months notice."

I tried a few words in my defence and pointed out that she was getting the gardening done as part of my contribution.

"I can do the fucking garden myself," she snarled.

I was beyond speech. I shut the door and went upstairs and sat, stunned, on the sofa staring out of the window, seeing nothing, feeling weak with shock. I hardly moved for the rest of the day, other than to crawl into bed. The morning came and I didn't go to work, just moved about, quietly, upstairs. At lunchtime I felt exhausted and went and sat on the sofa. My phone rang. It was one of my friends. She wanted to know how I was settling in. There was a brief silence at the other end of the phone when I told her what had happened the day before, and that I was, in effect, being evicted. I am blessed with the most wonderful friends. My friend said that I must not stay there in that terrible atmosphere, but get out immediately. I could go and stay with her. The cats were going to be a problem now though, as my friends house was very artistically full of all manner of ornaments. She did, initially, say that I could bring them, but I knew cats, and this friend had not, to my knowledge, ever kept pets. I would have to find them a temporary home. I couldn't afford a boarding cattery and trusted that my situation would soon be resolved. I had only one option and this was my former landlady from when I had the shop and who had always coveted Minerva.

I rang her and explained my dilemma. She said that she would look after the cats for me. I was to provide food for my three and also some extra cat litter, to help with the cost. I didn't seem to have much choice. I did have a choice, I could have found them homes but I didn't think that it was necessary. Once these arrangements were in place, I started packing my things up. I gave all my house plants away, and some furniture, some bits I put for sale in a bric-a-brac shop, some things I took to the tip. Douglas came the following Saturday, and moved larger items that I was keeping back into the friend's garage, from where I had moved, them just over two months previously. Another friend came on Sunday and we worked tirelessly, moving the small boxes of books, and clothes that I could manage without, for the time being, back into my friend's garage. Last of all, I took the cats to the Dutch woman's house. I was very upset, I had a feeling that it would be difficult to get them back. I took a suitcase full of clothes to my friend's house. A lovely clean and comfortable bed had been made up for me, in a room that was spotlessly clean and didn't smell of smoke.

Chapter 50

My room was on the second floor of my friend's house and had a velux window. I left the blind open and watched the night sky drift over eventually falling into a troubled sleep, in the early hours of the morning. Despite the comfort, warmth and kindness. I had spent a restless night. Disturbing, remembered images came visiting in the darkness, my landlady's rage, her expression, her high colour. Leaving the cats with the Dutch woman. Getting rid of things that

I liked, but could manage without. I had sorted myself out in less than a week. It had been a muddle of trying to do some work and then taking time to pack things up. At work I had been hampered by horrible feelings of insecurity and waves of nausea. I had managed about an hour and then had to have a rest, before trying do a bit more, sometimes the nausea was too bad and I would have to go back to what was then my home. The cats had come to greet me when I walked in. I had cried and hugged them, knowing that once I parted with them, I might not get them back.

My friend slept in the room below, I could hear her radio. She had asked me to let her have first use of the bathroom, as she had to get off to work. I lay in bed, listening to the sounds of her morning routine and wondered where to begin unravelling the mess I was now in. I felt sick with nerves, but had to, at least try, to go to work. I had a cleaning job to go to in the town. One thing I was absolutely resolved not to do, was to go to my Doctor for anything to calm my nerves. I pondered on the fact that I had weathered a few months now of extreme stress, and I had not suffered an asthma attack. My mind wandered back to the breakdown that I had had many years before. I wondered about the possibility, that if I had known more about nutrition then, it may never need to have happened. I also wondered if I had been borderline "off my rocker" for most of my married life, as a result of malnutrition, while I lived mostly on a starvation diet, in order to try to stay slim.

The times when I had relaxed and ate more, to my horror, I could actually gain a stone in weight in a week.

My reverie was interrupted by my friend calling to let me know that the bathroom was free, and did I want a cup of tea? I put a dressing gown on and went downstairs. I had absolutely no idea what I would have done if she had not come to the rescue, but it was a temporary solution, as she always had friends that came to stay with her during the T.T race weeks. That meant that I had until mid May to find somewhere else. Having by this time, been thoroughly frightened by private rental situations, my first port of call would be the Commissioners to see if there was anything that they could do to help me.

I decided not to go to work that day, I was too distracted, and there was too much on my mind. I needed a day to calm down and get things in perspective. I got myself my now essential cooked breakfast of bacon, eggs, and for good measure, some black pudding, accompanied by mushrooms. Whilst I had been living in this whirlwind of a trauma, I had kept rigidly to my eating plan and had resisted any comfort eating or drinking. Some days I had felt almost too sick to eat, and on these days, I had eaten very small amounts of meat or hard boiled egg at regular intervals, as frequently as every hour. Every time I felt nauseous I would try to eat, even if it was only a mouthful. I believe that it stopped me from caving in altogether.

Feeling much better, after having my first really good meal for several days, and relaxed, after having a soak in the bath. I got dressed and did my hair and put some makeup on. I always felt more equipped to face the world behind my makeup. Although the Commissioners were sympathetic to my plight,there was absolutely nothing that they could do to help me. If I had been a single parent, with a child, it would have been a different story. I was number 38 on the housing list, and I knew that the average wait was about six years. That would leave me with just over four years to go.

Next, I went and bought cat food and litter and phoned the Dutch woman to say that I would be calling round. The visit was distressing, the place was in it's usual, stinking state and the cats were, understandably, nervous. They came out when they realised that I was there. Too late, I realised that I had made a mistake.

Back at my friend's house, I was feeling more motivated than ever to write a self help booklet, in order to share my experience of what diet could do and, hopefully, help other people. I had begun jotting down some ideas on paper whist I was still at the Chapel, but was finding it very difficult. I considered that it might be an idea to go and see my doctor and tell him what had happened and that the stress had not triggered an asthma attack.

I was by no means out of the woods. I had had to take time off work, to get the upper rooms fit to move into in the Chapel, and had lost more time moving out. Today I didn't feel up to going to work. The estate car that I had bought the previous year was turning out to be another disaster. I had bought it without a guarantee and had found to my horror that the brakes were practically non existent. A front wheel hub and bearing had also needed replacing. It was possible that the vehicle had been accident damaged and should not have been resold. I was still trying to pay the mechanics bill for work done the previous November. Then there were the, now high, credit card bills, with added charges for late payments, payment protection insurance, and the ever increasing interest charges, the loan payments, critical health insurance payments on a policy that the bank thought it would be a good idea for me to have, and Denplan payments, as my dentist had gone mainly private and I was now in the Denplan scheme.

It was a relief to get back into my friend's house. I made myself a simple lunch of some salad and half price salmon fillet that I had bought at the supermarket. I sat in my friend's kitchen, mulling over what cutbacks I could make. The health insurance could be cancelled. My faith in dietary solutions to illness was very strong now. I would have to cancel my Denplan membership and sign up with a National Health dentist. Already I would be saving nearly £60 a month. The payment protection on the credit cards could be cancelled. It hadn't been of any use while I was in dire straights. I wrote to my dentist, and thanked her for all her patience and work on my teeth, and explained that I was in a financial fix and was having to make cutbacks, which meant that I would have to register with a National Health dentist. I wrote to the bank and cancelled my Critical Illness insurance. I had a phone call asking what I would do if I were to be come critically ill? With fingers crossed, I confidently assured the caller that I knew how to stay well. I rang the credit card companies and cancelled the payment protection insurance. That was all I could do for the time being, but it would save over a hundred pounds a month. All this had left me feeling drained. I headed upstairs to the peace and quiet of my room.

Chapter 51

On the landing at the top of the house, my friend had put a largish bookcase, crammed with all sorts of books, some serious, some frivolous, some stories. A funny little book caught my attention, *101 reasons why it is good to be a woman.* I sat on the top stair and flipped through it. It had one reason on a page and a cartoon drawing on most of the facing pages. The thought occurred to me that my self-help booklet could take a similar form. I could put one or two thoughts on a page and not overwhelm people with complex facts. I went into my room and pondered how to start. It still wasn't easy.

Everyday, I would spend a bit of time on my self-help booklet. It was slowly taking shape. I wrote to the company who had published the little book that had inspired me, and told them about the booklet that I was working on. I was about halfway through at this point. They invited me to send on to them what I was working on, which made me feel even more enthusiastic. A reply came back together with my half written offering saying that they might give it consideration if my doctor were to endorse what I had written, and, if I were to gain permission to make the quotes that I intended to use from Dr Abrahamson's book, "Body Mind and Sugar." I knew, without asking, that no doctor was going to endorse my booklet and decided to put it away, for the time,being, and concentrate on work. I still had to find my next temporary home, as, even with the cutbacks on my outlay, there was no way that I could even consider paying out on a private rental now. The eviction fiasco had nearly bankrupted me. It had also made me very nervous of private rentals. I went to most of my customers on a weekly basis. I was still doing some cleaning, so that even if the weather was bad, I still had some income.

Among these weekly customers were a couple, who lived in a farmhouse up in the hills. It was one of my favourite places to go. I had got to know the husband while I still ran the Health Food shop, he had a habit of calling into the shop late afternoon, and if he saw my landlady hanging around. He would come and rescue me by out staying her.

He was retired and not in the best of health, after having a kidney transplant. His wife, who was younger, still worked full time. Their's was my last call on a Friday, I would find some half price offering in the supermarket on the way up, and would make a meal out of it for the two of us. The meal became a weekly ritual that we both looked forward to, and had come about by accident. On one of the lists that his wife had left, there was an instruction that we were having great difficulty deciphering. It looked like, "Feel June". We thought this hilarious, but decided that it was more likely to be "Feed June!" After the feeding, we would then tackle whatever was on the wish list that his wife had left. Although, sometimes, her husband would have first claim on my time. This didn't always go down too well with his wife, as it was she who paid. However some compensation was gained by them, as I generally gave them far more time than had been paid for.

The previous year when I had been advertising for accommodation, he had said that, if the worst came to the worst there was always the former tack room. This was a small room, situated at the house end of a semi-derelict barn that ran side on to the road. The house was situated, gable end to the road, and the back door faced the short flight of concrete steps that led up to the tack room. I couldn't imagine that I would ever be reduced to camping out in this damp cobwebby room. Now though, it was beginning to look like I would be lucky to be given the option to use it. The offer was still there, and time was running out for me to find an alternative. It ran out. I had to swallow my pride and place myself at the mercy of these people. I am sure that it was every bit as difficult for the various people who ended up helping me as it was for me to accept help. I had always been proud and to find myself in such a humiliating situation was mind numbingly embarrassing.

May arrived and I still hadn't done anything about moving. Now I was beginning to have anxiety attacks, worrying about it. I had just got out of the bath one morning, and the unpleasant feeling of anxiety, panic and nausea swept over me. I sat wrapped in a towel not wanting to move. My mobile phone rang. It was the wife whose husband I enjoyed my Friday lunches with, and who left the lists of chores to be attended to. She asked how I was, and, reluctantly, I told her exactly how I was feeling. She then suggested the tack room. I assumed that they had talked the matter over and come to some agreement. She, being the professional one, put me at my ease and made it possible to accept the offer. The deal would be, that I could have the use of it, rent free, in return for making it fit for them to use as extra space for guests. I felt better almost immediately. It first had to be cleared of a lot of old papers that her husband had stored in there. He helped me with that. Most of it was rubbish that could be burnt. The bits of furniture we moved into the driest part of the old barn.

The race weeks were approaching very quickly. The room had been dry lined and then strips of paper had been put over the joints in the plasterboard. Most of these were hanging like streamers. I glued them back in place and emulsioned the walls. Douglas found me a piece of carpet in a lovely shade of blue. I put up a thick, chunky shelf, that I had had especially made, to provide a bit of extra storage when I lived at the little tiny cottage. I had got the local metal work shop to make me some wrought iron brackets to hold it up. It was starting to look good. I had a little metal curtain rail that I had bought, at some point, and not used. I put this up at the window and hung from it some silk curtains that I had made for somewhere and also not used. I had a single, tubular metal bed that I had used in the attic in the house that I had shared with Douglas. I put that width ways across my room, at the window end. In the tip I found a small, clean, chest of drawers, a small table and a quite nice television, also a useful little wall cupboard and one of those wooden kitchen thingummy's that doubles up as a wooden work surface, wine rack, shelves, and with one useful drawer. Douglas supplied a DVD player. I was set. When the bed was made up and I put my sapphire blue fleece throw on, it looked lovely. From the little window, I looked out over the valley towards Snaefell in the distance. There was electricity in this room and, to keep it dry, a dehumidifier needed to be on constantly.

The back door of the house opened into a small utility kitchen, and off that was a downstairs bathroom. The door from the utility kitchen, into the main house, was the original back door, and opened into the main kitchen. It could be locked at night. They would leave the outer back door unlocked so that I could have use of the bathroom in the night, should I need it. I would still carry on as before, working for them on Friday afternoons, and I would be paid for that. Everybody seemed happy. I bothered the family as little as possible and was reasonably content in my little place. As an extra thank you, I did other work around the place, for which I did not want payment.

It was during this summer, whilst I was living in the tack room, that Douglas told me that he had proposed to Julie and that she had accepted. They were going to be married at the end of July. I felt truly happy for him, that despite everything, he was managing to pull his life together and make sense of it. I was delighted that it was Julie that he was going to marry as I was very fond of her.

Chapter 52

Douglas would, from time to time, keep me informed of his father's antics. And it was just after I had closed the Health Food shop, that he told me that his father had married for a third time. This time, to an American woman whom he had impregnated. Not long after that, I heard that he had left this woman when the baby, a girl,was only a few weeks old, and gone back to his parents' home in Lancashire.

For the first time in 18 years, I felt compelled to get in touch with him, and sent a letter to his parents' home, urging him to, at least, try to mend bridges for the sake of the little girl. I pointed out that my childhood had been badly marred by the upheaval of my mother leaving my father, and the subsequent spin off.

To my great surprise, I got a very quick reply from him. He was delighted to hear from me and hoped that we would be able to keep in touch. This we did, as friends. He went back to America and the American wife, and I crossed my fingers and hoped that all would be well. I doubt that mygetting in touch with him had anything to do with his deciding to go back. In his letters, I got the impression that she was definitely 'the One' and he seemed thrilled with his situation.

Anyway, after a few years,they decided that they would like to go and live in Southern Ireland. This they did, but difficulties arose which resulted in his wife taking off, back to America, from time to time. Finally, she took off, apparently, for good. This was while I was still living with Douglas at the larger house. His Father said that he would love me to see the place that they had, in Ireland, where he was happy. Even more surprising for me was that I found that I really wanted to go, and made arrangements to go for a weekend, taking my dodgy car on the ferry to Belfast and then to drive down to Ballyheigue, where he had his "dream home" It did sound nice in his letters. Now, I am hopeless at finding my way around and out of strange cities. It took me 2 hours to get out of Belfast, and then I managed to take a wrong turning and go over a hundred miles in the wrong direction. We kept in touch by text, me saying what town I was going through, or approaching, and him replying, "Oh, Juney, you are miles off course!"

We had arranged to meet in Tralee, as there would be little hope of finding my way to his place (I could possibly have managed it if I had had a week to spare, to enable myself to get lost several times and spend a few nights in bed and breakfast accommodation). I arrived 6 hours later than I had expected, exhausted. Having come over on the night boat, and worked the previous day, and then driven all day. It felt both strange and pleasant to see him after many years. I followed him back, out of Tralee, along the country roads to the place that he was so fond of. It was not what I expected in any way, shape or form, but I was made very welcome and a bed had been made up for me in a spare room. Since our parting, he had pursued his musical interests and it had been whilst he had been touring and playing in America, that he had met wife number three.

He was due to be playing in a pub that evening, in a local town, and wanted me to go and watch. I did, and he sang his heart out. He later said that he was trying to impress me, but I was so tired I could have lain down on the floor and gone to sleep. It wasn't for me, the pub scene. Still we had two days together, and they were pleasant and because we had parted on bad terms, it was nice to have this interlude. I almost didn't want to go. With only a few hours left until I was due to leave, he suggested that I stayed, 'did a runner', and stayed for ever. Morality would always get in the way of me doing anything so rash and adventurous. For a start, he was still married and there would be a possibility that they might resolve their differences. Besides which, I did know him of old. Experience told me that it would be too big a risk to take and I said "I can't ", and burst into tears.

Chapter 53

I went back to the Isle of Man. They, my ex-husband and his wife, by some miracle, seemed able to carry on, yet again. So they were still together when Douglas was due to get married, and still in Ireland. But, they planned to go back to America on the actual day of his wedding. I thought it would have been so nice for Douglas to have had his father present and I pleaded with him to change his plans. Thinking, in my silly romantic head, that he would behave like a proper father and give his son some moral support. He said that he couldn't, because of the cost but eventually agreed to come over for a couple of days, beforehand. His wife chose not to come. Instead of giving Douglas a bit of a boost, which is what I had hoped for, he managed to upset and offend everyone, resulting in Douglas, Julie and his granddaughters wanting nothing more to do with him. I was very disappointed, and felt that it was my fault. After all, if he had been in the least bit interested in his son's welfare, I wouldn't have needed to prompt him to come over. He really was just the same as ever. We kept in touch but some of the restored gilt had worn off our friendship. He didn't seem to understand how he had managed to upset everyone.

During this somewhat surreal summer, I began getting phonecalls from a withheld number. When I answered the phone, the caller remained silent and then rang off. A couple of months passed with my getting these phonecalls from time to time. Then, one day,the caller spoke. It was my former landlady who had evicted me earlier in the year. She asked how I was, and I found it hard to be civil. I told her that she had almost bankrupted me, that I had had to part with my cats, most of my things, my considerable collection of house plants, had had to cancel my Critical Illness insurance, also my private dental insurance payments, and could now not afford dental treatment. She said that she was sorry and that her medication made her crazy, which didn't help my situation, other than I now knew that it wasn't my fault. She phoned me a few times more, and we always had the same conversation. She re-affirmed that her medication made her crazy. After a few months, she stopped phoning.

I always seemed to have a complication, waiting in the wings. This year was to be no exception. One day, I had rushed to finish work in a garden, so that I could get to the tip and drop off the green waste before they closed. Running up the steps to a higher level of the garden, to bring some bags of grass back to the car, I caught my foot on the top step and went sprawling on the brick patio, grazing the skin off my palms and elbows, the wounds ached and bled. I wrapped some tissue around them and hurried on.

Arriving at the tip, there was something new. A small skip was positioned with a sign in front, indicating that grass clippings were to be deposited in it. A private concern had started up an independent composting site nearby and they were now taking the green waste from the tip. One of the directors of the new company was standing by the skip, with one of the site operatives. As I opened the back of my car, the site worker said, "She's a business. She needs to pay." The other asked if that was correct, and I said that it was. I had just enough money in my purse to pay for dropping off the grass. I had intended to buy some pain killers before going on to another job, but now I would have to manage. On top of that, I would now have to take my green waste to the composting site, since I was "Commercial". This was the end of my customers' free tipping.

A man was employed to run the compost site. He was very friendly and it was always hard to get away. On top of that, through, being profoundly deaf, he had a speech impediment, which made it difficult to understand what he was saying, and he always had a lot to say. It was on one of my dropping off waste visits that he grabbed me and asked if I would go for a meal with him. If there is one thing that I absolutely hate, it is being grabbed. I had pushed him away, at the same time, reminding him that he had a girlfriend. I knew this, as he was always talking about her. As for the dinner invitation, it was a definite, "No, thankyou." Now I didn't want to go back there. My friends, up at the farm, said that I could take my green waste up there. It seemed like a good idea to stay away from the compost site for a while.

Chapter 54

The tackroom was another temporary home. I would not be able to use it over the winter months as the weather was more extreme at the higher altitude. I managed to brave it out until the second week in December, when, reluctantly, I had to admit defeat. Possibly, I would have managed to carry on camping there if it hadn't been for the door. The door was about twenty five years old, and had been a really sturdy door. While it wasn't in fact rotten, there were gaps, where the planks had split and opened, after years of weathering. When it rained, the rain came in through the gaps.

During the summer, when I had got the measure of my surroundings, it seemed to me that the only thing preventing my staying through the winter was the door. I asked my friends if they would be agreeable to me replacing it, at my expense, in order to stay on. They didn't mind at all, since it would make the room better for future guests.

From time to time, I would meet up with the man whose woodworking shop my "artist boyfriend" had worked in, part-time. We would have a coffee and or a snack and a general catchup. So the next time I met him, I asked if he could recommend anyone to make a door for me, for the tack room, saying that it didn't need to be a "Rolls Royce job." He decided that he would like to do it. He said that he fancied doing something different for a change. And with his cheery words, "Don't worry, I won't rip you off."I had put my trust in him, and arranged for him to call up to the farm the following week and measure for the new door. He was, however, a man who liked a drink, and he liked nothing better than to drink with people whom he considered to be of merit. So it was to my misfortune, that a certain radio presenter and his family had moved to the Island, to their misfortune that their relationship became fraught, and to my further misfortune that my friend, who was to construct the new door, became a drinking buddy of this man, now estranged from his family. This new friendship, between my door maker and his new, high profile friend, sprang up after our meeting over coffee, and before he came the following week, to measure for the door.

My friend, at the farm, and I were having our ritual lunch when the door maker friend arrived, late and noticeably hung over. He stood in the kitchen doorway, looking very pleased with himself "I didn't get home until gone three," he informed us, "I was out with," there then followed a suitably long significant pause.....It was apparent that he could hardly contain himself,

"ANDY KERSHAW." For him, it was a major coup. For us, it was of little interest. He couldn't set about measuring for the door until he had delivered a blow by blow account of his night out. We sat and listened. Eventually relieved of the excitement, he went off to do some measuring. This was mid summer. Autumn arrived and there was still no sign of my door. More annoyingly, I had paid him £600 as from time to time, he would ask for another interim payment, and each time I had given him a couple of hundred pounds. This had begun to worry me, as,during our initial conversation over a cup of coffee, he had mentioned a figure of £250. He called, yet again, and said that he needed another interim payment. This time I said that I needed to see an invoice before I gave him any more money. Now, December had arrived, and no sign of my door and no word from my "friend" since I had asked for an invoice.

I had arranged to spend the winter back with the first friend that I had stayed with, before my eviction. But before I went there, I had a house sitting job that would last for three weeks and would take me into the new year. I comforted myself with the idea that each day was a day nearer to my being allocated a local authority property. Though I still seemed to be number 38 on the list. I am glad that I did not know that I was to spend the next four years drifting from one temporary situation to another.

Despite all this to-ing and fro-ing, I carefully paid attention to what I ate. I still had no asthma and decided to pay my doctor another visit and tell him how well I was, and that the diet was still working. I don't know quite what my doctor made of me. He was always polite, and never dismissive, as the other doctor had been. He had also heard of Dr Abrahamson, but never seemed quite able to catch on to my enthusiasm for my return to health. To my disappointment, he just seemed pleased that the diet was working for me. He reminded me again that there were many different reasons why a person may become asthmatic. I pointed out that every other living creature on the planet, with the exception of human beings, knew what to eat and when to eat it. That they were all uniform size,and had no need for anti-biotics or hospitals and lived in harmony with nature. I went on to illustrate further, by pointing out that certain birds preferred nuts and seeds, while the blackbirds preferred worms.

Chapter 55

I had now finished my self-help booklet, apart from the illustrations that I still had to work on. I also needed to gain permission to make the quotes from Dr Abrahamson's book. A customer who had become a friend and who was used to dealing with media officials, red tape, and all the obstacles that could prevent my progress, came to my aid and tried, without success, to help with gaining these permissions, in order that I could include, what I felt were essential quotes from Dr Abrahamson's book, "Body, Mind and Sugar." Eventually we had to give up, my friend, suggested that, as I had been managing for so long now without an inhaler, that I didn't need to include the quotes, since I had proved beyond all reasonable doubt that the diet worked. I didn't have the confidence that this would work, since I was only a lay person, and it was only one person's experience. There wasn't enough weight behind it. I stopped thinking about completing my self-help booklet, and put my notes away. I felt relieved that I had absolved myself of the responsibility. Why should I care? It would appear that no-one was interested anyway. I would just carry on testing the diet on myself and noting anything of interest. Besides which, everyone was sick of my endlessly going on about nutrition.

My house sitting job involved looking after a delightful collie cross called Sam. It meant that he could stay at home whilst his owners had a holiday. I enjoyed the change, since work is quiet over Christmas and New Year. We had walks on the beach, and in the hills. I felt relaxed, since I no longer felt any inclination to raise public awareness, and the magic that could be achieved as a result of understanding nutrition. The three weeks passed, and I packed up my things and headed off to my next temporary stop. The strain was beginning to tell on me, but I was now very nervous of private landlords. I would have struggled to pay rent, as my outgoings now exceeded £1000 a month for the debt alone. That was before I bought petrol, food etc. I tried in vain, from time to time, to get a bank loan to pay off my credit cards, but was refused each time. I tried negotiating with the credit card companies to see if I could convert the borrowing to a loan, or even pay a reduced interest rate since I didn't use the cards now (initially I had used them to subsidise my business), but met with negative responses each time I tried.

Although I stayed rent free with the various people that I stayed with, I gave such a lot of time, by way of thank you's, that it was possible, that had I used the time for paid work, I could have afforded to pay rent. But then again, I was nervous of private landlords. I was also nervous of offending my friends. It was a "No Win" situation. Because I was useful, people seemed only too happy to have me stay, though, at times, I felt that my usefulness was being exploited. I moved back to the first friend's bungalow and prepared to live out of a suitcase for the winter. I was due to go back to the farm in the spring and stay in the tackroom again for the summer. This year, 2007, was the centenary of the T.T motor cycle races. The next complication was looming.

Suddenly, all my friends had friends who wanted to come over for the races. My friend at the bungalow had friends who wanted to come over for race week, the friends at the farm had extra guests coming for the race weeks, and they were going to use the newly refurbished tackroom as extra guest accommodation. Everyone, it seemed, had people coming to stay. I could go back to the tackroom after the race weeks, but in the meantime, I would have to move my things out as they needed to put a double bed in there. Just when I thought I had got my temporary accommodation sorted out indefinitely, fate had cast another pebble into the pool.

I had begun taking green waste back to the new composting site, since it was too far out of my way to take it up to the farm. I hadn't been there for six months and expected that the man would have found a distraction elsewhere. Alas, he had not. Even worse, it appeared that he had parted company with his girlfriend. Would I now like to go out for a drink with him? I said I wouldn't, as I wasn't keen on pubs. He said that he wasn't keen either, that he just went now and again to get out of the house. Silly me, I had begun to feel a bit sorry for him. He had such a lot of hard luck stories, about how his first wife had gone off with someone else, how his second wife had gone off with

another woman, about all the help he had given his various girlfriends, plus the cost out of his own pocket, only to be dumped in the end. He was beginning to sound like a hard done by saint.

I happened to be looking after Sam the collie again, when he asked again if we could meet up. I intended taking Sam for a long walk on the mountain the following Sunday. I said that he could come with me, if he wanted, on one condition and that being that he didn't grab me. He said that he would like to come along, and so we arranged to meet at the black hut on the mountain road the following Sunday.

It was my intention to quell his interest by showing him what I meant by long walks, sure to put him off. We crossed the mountain road and walked along the ridge to North Barrule, from there down into Cornaa valley, where we ate the lunch that I had brought along. I was getting used to his poor speech, though it was very trying having to repeat everything I said about four times, since he stubbornly refused to wear hearing aids. Lunch finished, we began to walk along the valley back towards the mountain road. This is a pretty strenuous walk and I took enormous pleasure in the fact that I was able to cope with it, thanks to my perseverance with the diet.

Not a day went by when I didn't think of my great good fortune in finding J.I. Rodale's book in the tip. The good health that I was now enjoying could not have been bought. It was a priceless compensation for the adversity that I felt that I had been up against for most of my life. My companion kept his word, and to my relief, didn't make any moves on me. Quite the reverse. He turned out to be very knowledgeable, and could explain what the ruined buildings in the valley had been used for, and how. It was to my surprise that I had had an enjoyable day. He wanted to meet up again. Tricky, I decided to persevere with the long walks. We walked along the railway line from Douglas to St John's, the millennium way from Sky Hill to Crosby. We went fishing in the sea, went to car boot sales, there seemed to be no putting him off. I said that I didn't like watching violence on T.V or at the cinema. He said that he didn't either.

My potential accommodation problem was looming, but I didn't feel like making any kind of romantic commitment. He kindly offered to let me stay at his home until my other bolt holes became available again. He admitted that he didn't really like walking, did like pubs, and did like watching violence on the T.V. We managed to stay friends.

Chapter 56

There were always other complications. The Dutch woman had had my cats for so long, that she had taken legal advice to see if she was entitled to keep them. She told me that she was prepared to go to Court over the matter. I could no longer deal with this and I gave up all hope of ever getting them back. I hadn't been to see them very often as I couldn't bear to see the conditions that they were being kept in. Worse still, I was powerless to do anything about it.

Meanwhile Douglas's father's third marriage had gone past the brink of no return and he was having difficulty finding work in Ireland, and couldn't meet his mortgage payments. He decided to look for work back on the Island, and found a job as a mechanic, without too much difficulty. So now he was in touch with me more often, and obviously not very happy. He had expected Douglas to put him up, but after the upset that he had caused at the time of the wedding, Douglas didn't want to know. Finally, he found somewhere to rent, but thought that the rent was too high and only stayed about three weeks before going back to Ireland. While we had been married, he had once said to me, "It's alright for you, you've always had money."He had had the experience, now, of having had some money, and of owning his own place, and now he was having the experience of having someone relieve him of it. It was a relief when he left.

Another year was rolling over, I still had lunch with my friend up in the hills on Fridays. His wife was due to go away for a short break, with their little girl. He was worried about a leaking water pipe underneath the concrete in the yard. They had their own independent water supply which came, via a spring, about two hundred yards away. He had rigged up a wonderful, Heath Robinson affair to catch the water with a series of pipes and old plastic water tanks, before it was pumped electrically up to the house. I suggested that my friend from the compost site may be able to fix it, as he was very practical, and he did love a challenge. I mentioned the problem to him and he said he would be only too pleased to go and deal with the leaking pipe, and arranged to come up the following afternoon, after he had finished work for the weekend at the compost site. I had to go and see a potential new customer in the afternoon, and I was also taking my friend's sister shopping. I said that I would go up, after I had taken his sister home.

It was November and a cold day. I had been getting complacent with my diet and had gone from feeling very insecure about living without inhalers, to being very confident. I hadn't had an asthma attack for years now, and the eating plan that I had devised was as far from Dr Abrahamson's original plan as it was from the eating habits that I grew up with. I found that I could go for six hours without a meal and not have an asthma attack. Dr Abrahamson would not have thought this possible. Anyway, I digress. By the time I dropped his sister off and got up to the farm it was 4.00 p.m. The light was fading and it was now very cold. My friend was still beavering away, breaking the concrete. As is the habit with water, the place where it appeared was not where the leak was, and he had to keep breaking more and more concrete away, further up the pipeline. It had now gone dark, and we had to shine torches on to where he was working. Eventually the leak was located and a repair was done, cobbling together all manner of redundant odds and ends that the friend with the problem had, in his Aladdin's cave of a workshop. The repair was finally finished by around 8.30 p.m and we went inside for a cup of tea. I hadn't eaten since breakfast. The farmhouse was freezing, as it was my friend's habit to turn the heating off when his wife was away, in order to save some of the heating cost. I was beyond cold. It was going on for 10.00 p.m when we left.

All I wanted to do, the next day, was sit in a chair with a hot water bottle. I didn't actually feel ill, but I didn't feel particularly well either. The next day, being Monday, I got ready for work. I still cleaned the house of the woman who had been my first customer after I had given up the shop. I had become a bit wheezy and suspected that it would be to do with getting so cold on the Saturday. Whilst I had, on the whole,been relatively careful about my diet, most winters, I usually had one bout of "bronchitis" or "flu" which had then "gone" to my chest. This usually lasted four or five days, and each time, I had chosen not to go to the doctor, since I didn't want to be given an inhaler or antibiotics. By Monday afternoon, I was struggling to keep going and was glad to finish and go "home". The wheezing was getting worse by the minute, but I comforted myself with the thought that I would be over it by the following week-end.

One of the biggest problems that I encountered, when I had these bouts of illness, was fending off the concern of my friends who would want me to go to the doctor's, whereas, I wanted to experience the illness, in order to understand more about it. Having got home, I was desperate to go to bed and lie down in comfort, but I found that when I lay down. I couldn't breathe. If I sat in a chair and leaned back, I couldn't breathe. The only way I could breathe was by leaning forward, and then only with great difficulty. I ended up lying face down with the pillows under my chest and my head lowered, sometimes, on my elbows and knees, hour after hour, gasping for breath. I was certain that an inhaler would not have relieved this condition. It was not an asthma attack. I wondered if I had pneumonia. I had heard of several people being taken into hospital at this time with pneumonia. Morning arrived and I determined that I must carry on with my eating plan. I had my cooked protein breakfast of bacon, egg and some baked beans with an onion. No bread or toast. Going to work was not an option. Fortunately for me, the friend that I was staying with, at this time was out at work during the day, and would not be aware of the state I was in. By the time they got back I would have retreated to my room.

I filled a hot water bottle and sat hunched over it, leaning forward in a chair. All I could manage were periodic visits to the kitchen and the bathroom. On the way home, the previous day, I had bought cold and flu relief powders and over the counter medicine to relieve bronchial congestion. Neither gave the slightest relief, but I carried on taking them, as one does, in the hope, that at some point, they would make a difference. Day after day I carried on. Spending the nights either laying face down or on my elbows and knees, struggling to breathe. The days were spent hunched in a chair, with a hot water bottle. A week went by. The following Monday I felt a little better and decided to go to work. It was lucky that I was working in an empty house, as I am quite sure that if the owner had seen the state that I was in, I would have been sent home. The day's work exhausted me and I was back to square one, healthwise. Possibly, even worse. I installed myself in my room when I got home. I had insisted that, on no account, was a doctor to be called. It was to my great relief that they did not argue the point.

This went on for roughly eight weeks. I wondered why I hadn't died. It seemed remarkable how ill a person could become and then exist in a critical state, with little change. I began to get better. I hadn't taken any antibiotics and had given up with the over-the-counter medicines after the first two weeks. I could no longer afford to buy them anyway. By coincidence, the people who had been hospitalised with pneumonia were ill for roughly the same length of time.

Chapter 57

During the time that I was ill, I did manage very small amounts of work, from time to time, and was able to pay my mobile phone bill and buy some food and petrol. I couldn't pay the credit card bills. The phone calls started. I told them that I was ill and had no money. They, however, wanted some kind of payment, however small. I argued with them that, had my borrowing been converted to a loan several years ago, there wouldn't be a problem now. This, of course, was irrelevant. To make matters worse, it was usually an Indian sounding agent on the other end of the phone. I did manage to get the interest frozen on the debts temporarily, but that was all.

By this time, I was starting to get bloody minded about my situation. I like to think that I am, at heart, a patient person, but my patience was wearing thin. I begged use of a friend's computer and checked my credit rating with Experian. There were companies on the website that I could contact about my debt problem. I decided to go into a debt management programme. This was, in fact, the last thing that I wanted to do. I would have preferred to clear my debts, without resorting to this measure, but as I was now in my late 50's, I could see that there was little hope of my achieving this. On top of that, I had now been on the local authority housing list for about four years. The average wait, I knew, was about six years. If, by some stroke of great good fortune, I was to be allocated a property sooner, rather than later, I doubted that I would be able to afford to pay the rent, given the amount of money that was going out on my credit cards. This was the thought that finally prompted me to seek help.

I got in touch with a debt management company and received the relevant paper work. Unfortunately though, the person allocated to dealing with my case was an Indian gentleman. It wasn't his fault, he was probably a nice person, but after my experience at the Indian restaurant I found that I couldn't deal with this man. I tried another company and this time was allocated an agent who sounded English. The first few months of going into a debt management programme can be a bit of a bumpy ride. The credit card companies are not going to be able to charge any more interest on the outstanding money owed, but since they had had thousands and thousands of pounds, out of me, they had had more than their pound of flesh anyway. With this step, I managed to reduce my out goings by over £800 a month. Looking back, I don't know how I had managed to keep on paying so much for so long.

I checked my position on the housing list again. Still number 38. The Housing Officer rang me and suggested that if I were to change to the waiting list for one bedroomed properties. I might be allocated a property sooner. I explained that the reason I had applied for a two bedroom property, was in case my mother, who was not in the best of health, decided to come and live with me. He said, should this situation arise, that my mother should come and stay with me and we could then be rehoused in a suitable property. I, then, on his recommendation, went on to the list for one bedroomed properties.

When a person goes into a debt management programme, they will not be able to have any borrowing for some considerable time. I hoped that I would not need any. But I did trundle around in a rather dodgy car. I kept it regularly serviced, kept a check on the oil etc. But then, one day when I was driving to my last job, and musing how much I loved this car with it's comfortable seats with the dralon covers, it's radio that automatically retuned itself, the sunroof.... I pulled into the driveway of the customer's house and parked. Getting out, I noticed a tell-tale semi-circle of oil following the line of my entry into the drive, and ending in a pool under the car engine. Oh no! I lifted the bonnet. A large rubber hose going into the engine had ruptured. My friend from the compost site came out and cut a piece off and rejoined it. I managed to drive home. The bad news was that the car had gasped it's last. I was very sad.

But then there was some good news, this being that, when I was getting rid of my things after the eviction, I had given a painting to a friend of mine. Given, because, at the time, she couldn't afford to buy it. When some time later she got back on her feet, and was buying a new car, she offered me her old one as a thank you for the painting. This was just a few weeks before my Citroen broke down, for good. I phoned, told her what had happened, and asked if she still felt the same about letting me have her old car, fingers crossed. I was desperate. It was alright. I could pick the car up the next day. Big sigh of relief.

The next day, the brother of my compost site friend towed me to the scrap yard that was taking my car. I did get some money for it but can't remember how much. Later that day, I went to pick up my next vehicle, from my friend who I have always called "darling Ruth". We met up at the place where she had her old car parked up. She had one little, last, short drive in it before handing me the keys and log book. I could see that she was sad to part with it, though she insisted that she preferred to have the painting.

Chapter 58

My new car was a little sports car, quite old but with mercifully low mileage. A Vauxhall Tigre, one of the ones with the long sloping back window, which meant that it had a remarkably large boot. At this time, I was still using a lawn mower that I could just push along (petrol, but not geared). I used to fold the handle down, to put it into the back of the estate car. Luckily, with the handle folded down, it would fit into the back of the Tigre, along with a set of ladders, a strimmer, a fork, spade, grass rake, ordinary rake, broom, coal shovel, hedge trimmer, extension cable and an assortment of hand tools. Once again, I was in a position to carry on.

I only had four cleaning jobs now, there was my "Darling Ruth", who had been my first customer, a very elderly couple, a very elderly friend of their's who was a widow and my friend who owned the bungalow where I had stayed before my move to the chapel, and again, when I needed somewhere to stay during the winter after leaving the tackroom.

I hadn't had much experience of death in my lifetime. There had been the sudden death of my grandfather, then my grandmother's death some eight months after the motor accident. One of my close friends had died in her early forties. She had cancer, but actually died from pneumonia when her immune system broke down.

The following summer, I was in for quite a few shocks. Firstly, the husband of one of my customers died suddenly, on the day that he was due to begin treatment for a brain tumour. A month later, my friend at the farm, where I had stayed in the tackroom, also died of cancer. The elderly widow, whose house I cleaned, died the following month. The next month, one of the first friends that I had made on the Island was found dead by her boyfriend. This one caused me terrible distress, as some time previously we had had a fall out, which had not been resolved. Then, at the end of the year, the husband of the elderly couple that I helped, died after a stroke. His wife died about six weeks later. I seemed to have been attending a funeral almost every month. It left me feeling very shaken.

I decided not to look for any more cleaning work after losing these customers, but to try to take up the spare hours that I had, with more gardening. This proved not to be too difficult. The little blue car served me very well, was reliable, and a source of great amusement to my customers who watched, with amazement, the unloading of many tools from the boot. The only draw back being, that I had to take all the long tools out, before I could lift out the lawnmower. This was difficult to do, as it first had to be lifted up, and then over the back of the boot. But I managed. The work that I did made me strong.

The following summer, I managed to get a very reasonable, second hand van. One of my customers gave me a lawnmower that they no longer used. It was a joy, an easy start and had gears as well. This made a wonderful difference to me. I kept the little sports car. It was a luxury that I couldn't really afford. This I justified by saying that it was useful to have a back up vehicle, in case the van broke down.

Life swallowed me up again. I began to get used to the spaces in my world that the deaths of my friends had left, though I would never forget any of them.

Chapter 59

Through my friend from the compost site, I met his elderly uncle and aunt who lived next door but one to him. It was through the uncle that I was re-introduced to the card game of whist. I had been taught to play whist by my grandparents, but had never thought to go to a whist drive. This had a lot to do with my grandmother, once recounting to me her experience at a whist drive, when she had committed the ultimate crime of trumping her partner's ace! The partner had apparently been furious. Just the thought of making a slip, and the resultant aggravation was enough to put me off. Until, that is, the lady who regularly took the uncle to the whist drives had a stroke. A bad one that was going to take a lot of getting over. So the uncle, who did not drive, was not able to attend the whist drives, which he greatly enjoyed. I said that I would take him. I was made so welcome, and wished I had known what fun these evenings could be. Before long, I was going to three whist drives a week, sometimes four. There were a few people who took the cards very seriously and couldn't bear to lose, but on the whole, it was a jolly, lighthearted evening out. I made a lot of new friends. The lady who had been so incapacitated after her stroke, made a remarkable recovery and it wasn't long before she was coming out again as well.

My wanderings continued. I reckoned that in about six months time I would be close to being allocated a property. My friend with the bungalow kindly said that I could spend these last few months with her. The dormer in her bungalow had been converted into a small, but serviceable flat, and she offered me the use of this until I was housed. Very grateful, I borrowed a carpet shampooer and cleaned the carpets, plus the hallway carpet downstairs. There was a tiny table top fridge in the living/dining room of the flat which wasn't working. I offered to replace this, since there was just room for a slimline fridge in the tiny kitchen. In the tiny bathroom there was just a sink and w.c, but I had a very attractive set, that my son had rescued from a house that he had been working in, and which had seemed too good to throw out. I had intended putting it in my bathroom when I got a place, but offered it to my friend instead. She seemed happy to have it, and arranged for a plumber to come and install it.

Then she became anxious about the sitting room furniture, which admittedly wasn't too comfortable. I was perfectly happy with it, it was so nice to have a bit of space. However, there was no reassuring her and she bought a beautiful, small second hand sofa. I took the other items to the tip. And yes, the little flat was very comfortable. In the bedroom was a small shower, oddly placed, as it's location prevented the door of the built in wardrobe opening fully. I was happy enough. It was nice to think that I was going to have this very comfortable, last six months or so after my six years of drifting. I relaxed, was happy in my work, and happy in the thought that each day was a day nearer to having a place of my own.

December arrived, my friend had begun to say, from time to time, that she wished that I didn't have to go. I felt uncomfortable with this and wished that she wouldn't. But persist she did, finally offering me the use of the flat for the rest of her life, and then the bungalow for the rest of my life, which was later changed to, as long as I needed it. I now found myself in a very awkward situation, and said that I would not be changing my plan. It was plain that the offer was made on account of my usefulness, though I did know that my friend was fond of me, as I was of her. The offer was made again, with my friend insisting that I would be far better off staying with her than having my own place. When it became clear to my friend that I was not going to change my mind, she became hysterical and accused me of throwing her kindness back in her face, also suggesting that I was mentally unstable. After that exchange, I did feel mentally unstable.

I had to go to work, but resolved, on the way, to call at the Commissioners' office. I asked if I had made any progress on the housing list. The receptionist said that the housing officer was in and that she would buzz him to come and have a word with me.

He seemed surprised to see me, and asked if I had heard something? I said I hadn't and asked why. He told me that they were just about to contact me, as a suitable property had become available. I could have cried with relief. I asked when I could expect to be able to move into the property and was told that it would probably be at the end of December. They just had to check it first.

Chapter 60

I went to work that day with a much lighter heart, but then began to dread going back to the flat. When I got home, my friend met me in the hall in tears, and to give her credit, she did apologise and say that some of the things that she had said to me in the morning were unforgiveable.

I took a deep breath, and told her that I had called at the Commissioners' office, on the way to work, and found that, by coincidence, they were about to get in touch with me, as a suitable property had become available. My friend's demeanour changed instantly, and I was accused of going into the offices and making a scene. I went, miserably upstairs to the flat, which now felt like a prison, which is what I felt that it would have been, had I agreed to stay.

I sat on the sofa, feeling utterly dejected, similar to how I had felt when my landlady at the chapel had decided to evict me. The one had been screaming at me to get out, the other, hysterical because I wouldn't stay. My "friend" was going to spend Christmas with her daughter, I was leaving the next day to do three week's house sitting, which would last until the end of the first week in January. It looked like I would be able to go straight from the house sitting into my home.

In the meantime,my "friend" and I existed in an uncomfortable atmosphere of strained politeness. The day of her departure arrived. Mine was the next day, and it was a relief to get to my house sitting commitment. On the second evening though, I began to have severe anxiety attacks and realised that I couldn't face going back into the bungalow, not even to get my things. I phoned my friend Ruth and asked if she knew of anywhere that I could store my belongings, that it would only be for about three weeks as I should have the key for my house at the end of December. Ruth said I could put my boxes of small stuff in her office, and that her mother, she was sure, would let me put my few items of furniture in her garage. I arranged to do the moving on the 27th. Most of my things were still in boxes, since there wasn't actually room in the flat, to put things like books, hang my few pictures etc. I was so glad that I had my van. I made an early start, and took all the tools out of the van. The weather was kind, dry and mild. Lucky again. I drove over to the flat. Just going into the bungalow now made me feel nauseous. Still, I had to get on. I filled the van with heavy boxes full of books,cursing my habit for collecting them. I took about three van loads down to Ruth's office, full of anxiety driven energy. Ruth's sister-in-law kindly came and helped with the furniture. Then I set to and cleaned the flat until it was spotless. I wrote a note to my friend, explaining that I had decided to move my things out in order to avoid any more unpleasantness. I wrote a similar note to her son, explaining that my housing authority house was expected to be ready at the end of December, but that I had moved out now because I could not face any more conflict. I dropped the note off, along with my key and went back to the house that I was looking after. I felt a huge sense of relief, and had no more anxiety attacks.

I waited until the New Year before contacting the Commissioners to see how soon I could have the key to my house. I still didn't even know where it was. I was afraid to ask. All that mattered was that somewhere, in Peel, a house was waiting for me. It even had a garden. I had tentatively mentioned to the Commissioners, some years previously, that should a situation arise where someone was in a property with a garden, who would prefer to be in one without, I would love to have a garden.

Ah, now I had a new dilemma. The house wouldn't be ready for a while, as it needed some refurbishment. Again, I was hesitant to enquire further. I rang my other fantastic friend, Greeba. It was Greeba that had helped me to move out of the flat at the chapel. She invited me to use a flat that she had, that was empty. I was so relieved and so grateful, but now I had become nervous of damaging my friendship with Greeba, since she hadn't wanted me to give her any rent. She was on holiday at the time, but once in the flat I felt too uncomfortable to stay, and so accepted an invitation from the widow of my friend at the farm to go and stay there until my house was ready. So, a week after moving into the flat, I moved up to the farm. But not into the tackroom, as it had become full of stuff. It had it's new door, fitted almost a year after I had first requested it, with another £400.00 additional cost. It seemed to have escaped that friend's notice that I was broke and homeless. He got paid but I fell out with him. It was a 'Rolls Royce' door after all.

When I was in Greeba's flat, I was beginning to become ill. It seemed like it was a bout of bronchitis starting. I hadn't had any illness since the severe one I had had, two winters previously. People I knew were quick to put this latest bout of illness down to stress. I must admit, I was puzzled by it, as since the experience that I had had two years previously, I had been very careful with my diet. Within a couple of

212

days of moving up to the farm, I had become very ill and not fit to work. My friend wanted me to see a doctor, which I declined, and did what I had done before, and kept out of the way.

This bout of illness was worse than the one that I had had two years previously, I was having great difficulty breathing, and was very weak. If I went downstairs, going back to my room was slow progress, as I could only manage two or three of the stairs at a time, when I would have to pause for a while, before I had the strength to carry on. I became very depressed. I was too ill to work. Though from time to time, I would feel slightly stronger and would manage a few hours work, the same as before. Also, the same as before, this would exhaust me. There was another aspect of the "illness" that I have not hitherto mentioned and that was that I was given to coughing up salty, frothy fluid. This time it was worse. I coughed up nearly as much as I tried to drink, and was "passing" very little fluid. My breathing was chronically bad. My lower legs took on a purplish hue and filled with fluid. The skin was dry and itchy. Another month went by. All I could do was rest and hope that, before long, I would start to improve. There are always clues, however, and how we interpret them depends largely on the situation in which they occur.

The experience took me back to my childhood and my frequent bouts of illness. I sat on the end of my bed and looked out over the fields and valley. Now I was starting to worry, that, when my house was ready, I wouldn't be well enough to work and how would I manage to pay the rent, let alone furnish it?

Chapter 61

My mother would phone from time to time. It was during one of these phone calls that we touched on the subject of the youngest of my two brothers. Of his two children, the youngest, a boy, had been born with a severe congestion, caused by a twisted gut. He had an emergency colostomy operation, in which half of his gut was removed, leaving him with just enough to survive. It was then hoped that the gut would settle down and be rejoined, dispensing with the colostomy bag. The operation to do this was repeated over and over again, without success. He was also prone to bouts of severe illness. The little boy spent the whole of the first year of his life in hospital, the family living in the hospital with him all that time. I said to my mother that I was surprised that the child hadn't been diagnosed as having been born with cystic fibrosis. She told me that he had been tested twice, but that each time the tests had given a negative result. After this his parents had asked to be tested. But their consultant advised them that there was no point, since there was no history of it in the family.

It was whilst I was ill at this time that it occurred to me to read more about cystic fibrosis. So I decided to check the symptoms and read more about it on the Internet. I was in for a shock, that shock being that I had lived with at least fifteen symptoms of cystic fibrosis for most of my life. This made me feel very sad. But it also helped me to understand why I had never felt properly

well, why I had such difficulties with my weight, insomnia, joint problems, edema, heart murmur, fatigue..etc etc. There was also a physical clue in the form of my club toes, maybe not grossly clubbed, but still, unmistakably, clubbed.

I thought there would be no harm in going to see my doctor. I wrote a numbered list of all the symptoms I had experienced and when and how, and made an appointment. I also took details of my nephew's condition and a photograph. By the time I got an appointment to see my doctor, mycurrent illness had eased a little. He was, as always, so kind. He allowed me to fully put him in the picture, and when I had done so, he remarked that he was surprised that cystic fibrosis hadn't been considered a possible cause of my problems before. He said that he would arrange for me to see a Consultant at Noble's Hospital with a view to my having a test to see if there was a hereditary problem in the family.

Meanwhile, I carried on. I was still baffled by my current bout of illness and determined to see if it could be resolved, or I would die trying. One thing that had begun to puzzle me about Dr Abrahamson's diet, to "neutralise hyperinsulinism", or "low blood sugar" (given that that is what he believed was the sole cause of asthma), was that after having indicated that salt (and potassium) are bad for asthmatics, he then recommended a breakfast with bacon or ham, both of which are salty meats.

Everything that is processed has a high salt content. And I was coughing up all this salty fluid, and then there was the discolouration on my lower legs. Was I poisoning myself with salt? There was only one thing to do, and that was to cut it out. I sometimes used garlic puree, in cooking for added flavour. On checking the label, yes,there was salt in that. Dr Abrahamson recommended cheese as well, salt in that. I used to use, from time to time, tinned salmon. Checking the label I saw that it had a high salt content. I would still go along with his theory about low blood sugar, as that "did appear" to be the root cause of a lot of my problems.

Shortly after this epiphany, I got word to say that I would have the key to my house in the third week in April. This was 2011. I was flat broke, but slowly getting better. Cutting out the salt had begun to have an immediate effect.

I still didn't know where the house was. I had been afraid to ask. Time I did. How lucky was I. It was old, built in 1906, a former almshouse, now divided into two properties, with a garden at the rear and views out over the former fish yards to Peel Hill. A new kitchen had had to be installed and a new bathroom. The rest of the property was in a poor state. I didn't mind, I was just so very, very grateful, and just in time, as I had totally outstayed my welcome at the farm, having been little short of useless.

I had picked up oddments of carpet at the tip, which I thought would do temporarily as floor covering. But Douglas decided otherwise and insisted on buying carpet for the whole house, and then took a week off work, to get me moved in, and make one room, at least, fit to use. The grubby paper was stripped off the living room walls and the woodwork painted, this, so that he could put the carpet down. The bedroom walls were stripped, washed and sanded, the flaking paint was scraped off the ceiling, cracks were filled, his step-daughter came along and did her bit. We painted the bedroom, and the carpet was put down. My things were retrieved from Ruth's office and her mother's garage. I put my belongings into my cupboards. It felt very nice to be re-united with them. My mother lent me £1000 and I bought myself one luxury, a leather bed that was slightly damaged and marked down to half price, probably not necessary but I craved just one luxury, after the years of drifting. The fact that I couldn't afford a mattress for it seemed of little consequence. Douglas suggested a blow

-up one, as a temporary measure, and brought one over, that he happened to have. It was amazingly comfortable. I put a mattress topper over it and couldn't have wished for better. I bought the minimum amount of oil for the oil tank, arranged for a key meter for the electricity supply, and generally slipped up a gear. All the time I was getting stronger. I had moved away now from Dr Abrahamson's dietary recommendations, and would think nothing of having a steak for breakfast, or a pork chop, or roast chicken or lamb.

Chapter 62

Two years previously, when I had, had one of my "surges" of wanting to raise public awareness regarding the possibility of controlling asthma by diet alone, I had approached the editor of the little free monthly magazine, "Manx Tails". I told him my story, and asked if he would be interested on publishing an article on the subject. He said he would, and so I had written an introductory piece, given my experience and recommended further reading of Dr Abrahamson's book and also J. I. Rodale's *Health Treasury*.

Just about everyone I knew got in touch, to say that they had read the article. People stopped me in the street to ask me what they should cut out. Alas, though, when I said that it wasn't quite that simple, and then went on at length about low blood sugar, and the myriad problems that it could trigger. (This according to Dr Abrahamson, who indicated that low blood sugar was responsible for triggering not only asthma, but also heart ailments, brain tumour, epilepsy, gall bladder disease, chronic fatigue, allergies, appendicitis, hysteria and every sort of neurosis), interest was lost immediately. Everyone, it would seem, was only interested in shortcuts.

However, now,with my experience with what I am going to describe as "salt poisoning," I am so relieved that I did not manage to publish my self-help booklet. Aside from the fact that no one seems to want to take responsibility for their own well being, I was beginning to have a niggling doubt about Dr Abrahamson's advice and theory, though it was Dr Abrahamson's research that set me on this course in the first place. Without that, I am pretty sure that I would have been an invalid by this stage of my life.

In the summer, I got notification to attend a hospital appointment to see a consultant. My own doctor, had suggested that I took with me the list of symptoms that I had experienced and typed out, and also a photograph of my nephew and details of his condition.

The hospital requested that I bring a list of the medication that I was taking, which was none. By the time I met the consultant, I was fully recovered, had revised my diet further, and was feeling very well. I can appreciate his reaction, to this seemingly very well person suggesting that she had been born with cystic fibrosis. I tried to explain that my concern was for my nephew and that I suspected that I may have been born with a lot of health problems etc etc... Having checked first symptoms on the Internet. "Huh, the Internet!" was his disdainful reaction. He told me that there was no way that I had been born with cystic fibrosis. For a start, I would not have lived this long. That I had lived this long was actually a surprise to me. I had expected to die the previous winter. He seemed thoroughly irritated by me and said that he would not test me for cystic fibrosis. I began to feel very nervous, and suggested that he was finding me irritating. This seemed to surprise him somewhat. He looked at the list that I had given him, then at his notes. He said that he was asthmatic and asked me what I thought caused the problem. I mentioned Dr Abrahamson and said that the condition was triggered by low blood sugar brought about by the pancreas being over-stimulated. This seemed to annoy him still further. He thought the idea preposterous, and that any doctor making such a claim was a crank. I became so nervous, I could hardly string a sentence together. I managed to tell him that the only reason that I was in good health was because I was on a very restricted diet. He looked at his notes again. We had stopped talking about my nephew, it seemed like I was on a hiding to nowhere.

I lapsed into thought. I didn't think that Dr Abrahamson was a crank. I think he was a totally sincere and dedicated doctor, who spent many years searching for solutions. And he had got results which he took great pains to write about. His research was helped by other doctors who had, decades previously, devoted themselves to research and wrote about their findings. It was his research and subsequent book that changed my life. How could anyone deny this? I was living proof that it worked and I had had so much wrong with me.

He noted that I had not used an inhaler for nine years, and then suggested that I was in denial about my asthma. Then he decided that he would listen to my chest. My breathing showed my lungs to be perfectly clear. He began to take a little more interest. He noted that the heart murmur was no longer there. He finished his examination and said that he would like to conduct some blood tests. I went in the next day and samples of blood were taken. Months went by and having heard nothing, I decided to go and see my own doctor. He had heard from the consultant. The blood tests had shown that I had above average levels of antibodies in my blood. This is consistent with someone that was prone to allergies and asthma. However, although the tests showed that I was still "allergic" to all the things that I had ever been allergic to, they also showed that I did not have any reactions. He did concede in his letter to my doctor that I seem to have achieved something remarkable with my diet. My doctor found this interesting. I said that it was a pity that more research hadn't been done, and he said that, due to the high cost, it would not have been possible to conduct a study, as I had done over such a long period of time, effectively, ten years now, 24 hours a day, 7 days a week, 365 days a year. It would seem, at this point, that there was nothing more to be said, so I thanked him for his time and patience and left.

Chapter 63

I decided, again, to just get on with my life. The garden at the back of my house had never been divided. I asked the Housing Officer about the possibility of having a fence, and was told that I could have a fence, so long as I paid for it, and so long as I left the few steps that led up to the raised area of the garden, on next door's side of the fence. It was late spring now, work was busy and I arranged for a man to come and give me a price. The price I was given seemed reasonable, and since I had been impressed by a fence that this man erected in a customer's garden, I asked him to go ahead. Meanwhile, I kept my fingers crossed that the weather would be kind, and that I would manage to scrape together enough money in time to pay for it. I did... Just.

Having the fence up made the place feel more mine. Now I had a new problem,and that was the fact that I was torn between going to work and staying "at home". There was an increasing amount of things that I could amuse myself with, here. More decorating inside, creating a garden outside. I had to be very disciplined and go to work. It wasn't really that much of a problem. I loved my job and found it an endless source of fascination, from the first spring flowers appearing, the frog spawn in the ponds, the bird life, to the summer flowers and the arrival of the migrating butterflies. There was another bonus, in the form of cuttings that I was able to take from choice plants in customers' gardens, and surplus from plants that needed to be divided, and plants that had seeded themselves and produced too many seedlings. Here I garnered more in the way of wild flowers, the foxgloves and aquilegia, the latter in a beautiful shade of blue. Friends and customers would donate other plants. All this was great, excepting that I hadn't got any space ready in the garden. The plants had to be housed temporarily in troughs and tubs. It would be so easy, at this point, to get carried away, enthusing about my home and garden, forgetting the whole point of this book!

So, to get back to the original topic. I feel that I have been massively compensated for the disappointments that have been visited on me, though, I confess, I think that they were largely of my own making, in the first place. I had taken the risks. A good outcome was not guaranteed. Now however, I had a home in which I could be safe for the rest of my life. I had good health, which,to me, was priceless beyond measure. I mused on the fact that if I were to be offered the choice of having my money back, at today's value, or, the knowledge that I have now. I would choose the knowledge, inasmuch that the knowledge is of far greater value. For a start it can't be taken away from me. It has made me feel self assured, more so, with each passing year, as I understood more clearly what the clues, generated by my study, were revealing.

I didn't mind in the least being "poor". Most of the time I found myself skating along by the seat of my pants financially. The amenity centre (tip) furnished me with most of what I needed, from a couple of comfy armchairs, to electric radiators, garden chairs, sink drainer, all manner of useful treasures. From time to time, in the charity shops, I managed to find useful items of clothing, just as much as I needed. Friends and customers gave me essentials for the house, a fridge, a cooker, curtains. So much was offered, I found myself having to turn some of it down or there would have been so much "stuff " in the house, there wouldn't have been room for me.

One thing about being relatively poor is that a person has to be more resourceful, always looking for cheaper ways to do things, and I enjoyed the challenge of this. My social life revolves around the whist drives which I find a constant fascination, on top of the many interesting people I meet at them. When time permitted, I would meet up with friends, or go for walks in the country.

But; not a single day passed when I didn't reflect on how well I felt. My health is better now than at anytime in my life, previously. When I leave my home, to go where ever I happen to be going, I am acutely aware of how comfortable

I feel "in my skin". When I walk, I am aware of how easy it is, to stand up straight. Walking is effortless, only a person who has known the opposite of this would be able to appreciate the difference.

I experienced many other unexpected benefits as a result of my restricted diet. My teeth, which had been weak, with chunks breaking off with alarming regularity, stopped breaking when I adopted my new eating habits. (This was very fortunate because now I hadn't been to a dentist for over eight years. I had begun to have work done on filling the gaps left by the teeth I lost after the restaurant fiasco, but had not been able to afford to have the work finished, and was left with a good bridge at one side of my mouth and a broken tooth and gaps at the other. My bottom teeth are also mostly broken). The awful sores on my face and legs healed and the itching stopped. I had no asthma or breathlessness.

I didn't get headaches. I had no hayfever. I was free of the constant nasal congestion. I no longer had a problem with low energy levels. I no longer sank into the severe bouts of depression that had been a problem for most of my life. I had very few menopausal symptoms, it was hardly noticeable. Illness took on a different form, from time to time. I might have a day or two feeling "a bit off ". It was only when I felt more my usual self again, it would occur to me that I had probably been a bit unwell for a few days.

One of the things that I had not been able to resolve with diet was the insomnia. I had weaned myself off sleeping tablets some sixteen years previously, but sadly for me, I had reverted to the way I was before. I had found a way of dealing with this, though, and Douglas fixed a television set on my bedroom wall and gave me a D.V.D player. When I went to bed, I would put on a favourite film and set the timer for an hour. I would always be asleep before the timer switched the set off. I would then be awake again, three hours later, but the same routine would usually get me back to sleep for a few more hours, and I was happy enough with that. The other thing that I had not been able to resolve with the diet was the tendency to bloating. I could see, just from looking at family photographs, that it was a hereditary problem. My grandfather had spent his whole life dieting, on and off, but always was stuck with the physique of a budda. He wasn't a greedy man, and worked incredibly hard. But nothing seemed to make any difference.

Another aspect of my changed health was the stamina. Being a gardener, I have to go with the flow, weather wise, sometimes working for two or three weeks without a break, getting time off when the weather was bad. I didn't, necessarily work eight hours a day, but a good part of the day would be taken up with work. However; sometimes, if the weather didn't break, I would have to take a few days off, as I would have managed to work myself to a standstill.

Chapter 64

Swiftly, on .....

At the end of the summer, I had a notion that it would be nice to be able to take a regular day off and to have some sort of interest with which to fill it. Not long after I had this idea. I happened to be looking at this and that on the local classified site. I browsed the miscellaneous column, and noticed that a riding stable in the North of the Island was "desperate for help." Hmmn... that sounded a bit too desperate for my liking, though I used to love riding, and had briefly had a pony during the time that my mother was married to my step-father. I looked again, a few days later. The advert was still there, and all they wanted was a bit of help on Saturdays, with the younger riders, walking the ponies on leading reins. In return for that was a ride. I was tempted, and a few days later I phoned and arranged to meet the woman who ran the stables.

I agreed to go the next Saturday. Most of the stable helpers, the predictable band of young girls, turned up at 8.00 a.m. Since I had quite a drive to get there, it was alright for me to arrive at 8.30.

Part of the reason that I had decided to go and help was out of curiosity, I had become very "allergic" to horses and I wanted to see if my diet had neutralised the problem. However, within a very short while of my having contact with the ponies, my nose began to stream and my eyes began to itch. In no time my cotton handkerchief was saturated. Only through a massive amount of will power I managed not to rub my eyes. By midday my chest was tightening up. I went and sat in my car and ate the cold meat that I had brought with me and some of the coffee. This eased the symptoms a little. But by 2.00 p.m I was wheezing and as a result of the wheezing, I was weakened and I knew that I would have to leave early. I was bitterly disappointed. By the time I got home, I was in quite a state. I had a bath and washed my hair, putting the clothes that I had worn straight into a bag. As soon as my hair was dry, I took them down to the launderette and washed and dried them.

The wheezing took hours to settle down. I was puzzled as to why this had happened. Could it possibly be a psychosomatic reaction? I had been heartbroken as a child when my pony had had to be sold, as I had never been able to properly get used to having him. The next Saturday arrived and I went along. I had my flask of coffee and some cold meat to have as a snack, plus plenty of handkerchiefs. I didn't want to take any antihistamine, as with my usual stubbornness, I wanted to see if there could be an alternative solution.

Again, my nose began to stream, and my eyes began to itch and I had to leave early when my breathing became difficult. Again, I was in a state when I got home. I felt a bit desperate and wondered if having something sweet might help, the sort of thing that might be given to someone in shock. I had a cup of very sweet coffee and a piece of cake. Then had a bath and washed my hair and took my clothes to the launderette and washed and dried them. The wheezing stopped in less than an hour. With this idea, I turned up at the stables the following Saturday, with a flask of sweet milky coffee and a piece of cake. As usual, my nose began to run, and my eyes itched, though I fancied that maybe it wasn't quite as bad as the first time. Come mid-day, I had my coffee and cake and found myself much improved and able to stay the whole afternoon. Each week, I had my hearty protein breakfast, my lunch of cake and coffee, and each week, unmistakably, I was becoming less sensitive to the ponies and better able to cope. By the end of eight weeks I could see that, in time, I would become tolerant. However I did seem to have landed myself with a problem, in that I was totally relied on, to be there every Saturday. Also, I was getting pretty tired, as the weather had been good and work had been busy. I still went to the whist drives, and I would work on Sundays to make up for taking the regular

Saturdays off. Predictably, I was going to hit the wall of exhaustion.

One of my customers remarked that I was looking very tired. I said that I was, and that helping at the stables had turned out to be a lot more involved than I had expected. Being older, I had ended up being given a lot more responsibility than just helping with the leading reins. I would be taking three or four rides out, some on foot, some on horseback. Still, I had enjoyed the rides. It was nice to find that I had not forgotten how to, and I had learnt more about asthmatic conditions, and have to concede to my doctor, that yes, there other reasons why a person may become asthmatic. Before I could give the owner of the stables some notice that I would be unable to carry on helping her, exhaustion overtook me and I ended up taking a week off work. I did offer to go back and help for another few weeks whilst she found someone else. But she said that it was O.K., and she found someone quickly. I wasn't that indispensable after all. Probably just very cheap.

In October, I received an appointment to attend the respiratory clinic at the hospital. It was required that I should undergo breathing tests. I duly turned up for my appointment, and was asked to sit in a cubicle, breathing into a spirometer. My breathing was monitored whilst I underwent various breathing exercises. After the first part of the test was completed, I was asked to use a ventolin inhaler. I found I didn't want to use it, but went ahead so that "they" could analyse what ever it was that the results showed. After I had had a ten minute rest, I went back into the cubicle and repeated the same breathing exercises again. This completed, I was free to go. I didn't feel any improvement after using the inhaler.

In December, I received an appointment to attend the respiratory clinic again. This time I was to see a consultant. A colleague of the one that I saw initially. I was able to ramble on for a while, about trying to help my family, in finding out whether or not there was possibly a hitherto undiagnosed problem with cystic fibrosis in the family. The consultant reassured me that I did not have cystic fibrosis. I pointed out that my current good health was entirely the result of a permanently restricted diet. He told me that I was an asthmatic, in remission, and went on to annoy me further by saying that should my asthma become a problem again more suitable inhalers could be prescribed. I repeated that the diet neutralised the asthma. He asked me what I had cut out, to which I replied that it wasn't that straight forward and couldn't be explained in a matter of minutes. However I gave him an idea of what I had cut out. As I spoke, I could see that he was not really interested.

We touched again, briefly, on the subject of cystic fibrosis, with him making the same comment as the first consultant had done, that I would not have lived this long. I suggested that maybe there would be the exception that would "test" the rule. I also mentioned the experience at the riding stable, but he didn't seem much interested.

Chapter 65

I waited a few months, and then went to see my own doctor, to see if he had heard from the hospital. He had had a letter from the consultant that I had seen. In his letter, he mentioned that I had mentioned the contact with horses, during which time "she felt that her eyes were streaming and that she had developed a mild wheeze, although this had now settled down." He mentioned my concern about the possibility of cystic fibrosis. But given the fact that I had no cough and my weight was stable, he thought that this was remote in the extreme. He said that the results of the tests that I had been given were consistent with a diagnosis of asthma, but that I was asymptomatic, and did not need any treatment at present. If, however, I was to need treatment, he said that he would only add a Salbutamol inhaler p.r.n. He mentioned that I was very resistant to the idea of an inhaler.

My doctor told me that the test results showed that after using the inhaler there was a 15% improvement in my breathing, though, as I mentioned, it was imperceptible to me. I suggested to my doctor that that was the end of it then, nothing more could be done? He affirmed this, and I said that it seemed such a shame, as so many people would be able to get some much out of life, if there were more information readily available. He said that there would have to be a cultural shift, if anything was ever to change; which was unlikely, as the majority of people would rather die, or pop a pill, or use an inhaler, before they would change their eating habits. I felt that I had done all I could do, and yet there was the constant reminder that I was well and others were not. I might be standing in a queue behind someone who was stooped and having difficulty breathing. I might be walking up a hill and pass someone who was struggling, in the same way that I used to. I might be sitting at a table at a whist drive, and be aware of the laboured breathing of someone else at the same table. I might hear of someone who had died during an asthma attack. Or I would have to sit and listen to people talking about "their" asthma, or people talking about someone being bi-polar, or this or that, and all these things Dr Abrahamson claimed could be neutralised with diet. All the time, I kept quiet. I was finished with promoting Dr Abrahamson's research. But, there didn't seem to be any peace for my mind. And so I decided to have one last go at raising public awareness. In order to give what I wrote, what I hoped, would be more weight, I would include a chunk of the history of my life, in order to illustrate how I came to understand the theory behind Dr Abrahamson's advice, how I found it to be flawed, and then spent years revising his dietary recommendations, and then spend more years testing my revisions on myself and noting the results. I began writing in December 2011, but had to give up in March, when work got busier and I found that I couldn't manage work and writing (and Whist).

Incidently, I had no winter illness in the winter of 2011/2012. No "flu" and no bronchitis. I had no colds or sore throats. I do not have vaccinations for either "flu" or pneumonia. Now putting the final touches to this work, it is March 2013 and I have had no illness this winter. I did have a very brief spell of the winter vomiting bug, very unpleasant, but it only lasted for four hours. I then spent one day resting and was recovered the following day.

In the meantime, I was to have yet to have another epiphany, possibly the most important one of all. In the summer of 2012, Douglas's marriage to Julie ended, the details of which are of no concern to anyone but themselves. However, Douglas suddenly found himself homeless, and after camping out for a few nights at various friends, he spent a week sleeping on my living room floor. He felt bad about this and very quickly got himself sorted out, with a most delightful and unusual place to live. It was during this time of his sorting himself out, that I saw a lot more of him. Previously not wanting to be constantly intruding on his marriage, I had seen the family from time to time, but not every week. The elder of my two granddaughters was now living with her boyfriend, and had invited us over for a meal one Sunday. She was turning out to be a lovely and caring homemaker and a very good cook. She had prepared a roast chicken with lots of trimmings, I took over a dessert. On this very restricted diet of mine, I do allow myself some treats, and if I go out for a meal, I enjoy it and tuck in. I do have a main course, and a dessert with cream, and cake as well, if there is cake to be had! Though I did keep off potatoes and bananas, once my favourites, now I had no interest in eating them. On this family gathering though, I said that I would have a little of everything, including the potatoes. (Dr Abrahamson's theory was tied up with asthma being the result of low blood sugar, brought about by the over consumption of simple carbohydrates. On this occasion, since I was certain that I had my blood sugar completely stabilised, one slip shouldn't upset the balance). My obsession with food had become the family joke, and invariably, when the family invited me over for a meal, to wind me up, they would say that there would be lots of potatoes....We had my dessert, which was a crumble with cream. My granddaughter had also made a banana cake (bananas are a food I avoid). After we had stuffed ourselves with everything else, I couldn't hurt her feelings by not trying her cake. It was delicious, I had another piece, and coffee with cream.

Even before I had finished my second piece of cake I was starting to get a bit wheezy. I was totally baffled. This couldn't be the result of my blood sugar dropping as, after eating carbohydrates or sugar in whatever form, the blood sugar will first rise. It takes time after that for it to drop to a level low enough to trigger a reaction, several hours (according to Dr Abrahamson), and it is when it reaches a crisis low level that symptoms begin to manifest themselves, being asthma, epilepsy, migraine, chronic fatigue, neurosis and insanity. Low blood sugar conditions have been found in people with suicidal and murderous tendencies.

No wonder that Dr Abrahamson had thought that he had found a golden key that would open many doors. But there was no way that I was suffering from low blood sugar so soon after finishing a meal. The house was spotlessly clean, so it couldn't be anything in the house. My granddaughter had recently acquired a little dog, but I was O.K with animals now (on the whole), and besides, it was one of those little dogs that are not supposed to trigger allergic reactions.

My breathing was getting worse by the minute, and the family were starting to panic. I asked them not to fuss and said that I had better go. My wheezing carried on, long after I got home, and for a while, the next day, I didn't feel too good.

Chapter 66

Finally, late in the afternoon of that day, and in the tenth year of my study of Dr Abrahamson's theory, of the root cause of most of the ills that beset our society, that being, low blood sugar or hyperinsulinism, to give it it's official title. I wondered if he had somehow missed a vital clue that his research had revealed, and that it was not low blood sugar that had triggered my asthma attack the previous day, but the sudden rise of potassium levels in my blood, as a result of my eating potatoes, parsnips, carrots and banana, all of which are high in potassium and are foods which are quickly digested allowing a "rush of potassium" into the blood stream?

In his book *Body, Mind and Sugar* Dr Abrahamson states that asthmatics tend to have excessive amounts of potassium in their blood, whereas the amounts of potassium in the blood of a diabetic tends to be low. In devising his diet, to stabilise low blood sugar, Dr Abrahamson found that he was able to neutralise both asthma and diabetes, but these two conditions are opposites, so how is it that a diet designed to stabilise blood sugar works for both? I now have doubts. What I think happened is that, yes, the diet did stabilise the blood sugar, which may have been fluctuating wildly, but the other thing that it stabilised was the potassium levels. The reason that these potassium rich foods triggered the asthma attack is because they are easily digested allowing potassium to be very quickly distributed through out the body by the blood stream. The conclusion that I am drawing, is that, although the body needs potassium, it cannot cope with a sudden rush of it, that, in sudden large amounts, I suspect that potassium becomes a poison. And now I am inclined to think that high levels of salt and potassium will cause breathing difficulties. Maybe, all the ailments that Dr. Abrahamson thought were caused by low blood sugar are actually symptoms of passive poisoning? Perhaps constantly high levels of salt and potassium in a person's blood, getting to unmanageably high levels, in tissue and flesh, are lethally poisonous.

Maybe coincidence enters into all of this, inasmuch as it makes it almost impossible to work out what is triggering what, and what, on the surface, may "appear" to be the obvious cause of a condition may turn out, in the end, to have little, or nothing to do with it.

I thought about my doctor's suggestion that in order for there to be any change there would need to be a "cultural" shift. But what if there has already been a cultural shift?, and that it has happened slowly over a long period of time. I am thinking about a span of about eight hundred years or more. From the times when the early explorers first began to bring back unusual foods from their voyages. The Romans it is thought introduced the vine to England around 2000 years ago, potatoes were introduced in 1536, bananas in the late 1600's. In hindsight it looks like each century heralded the arrival of more potassium rich simple carbohydrates, which in turn, would be embraced, and included in the diet of the time in ever more ingenious and interesting combinations.

I wonder what I am liberty to suggest here? I think that we like poisons, they taste so nice, we possibly don't have the slightest idea that we may be addicted to poisons, as it has happened so slowly over the span of centuries, do the ones that have the highest potassium content taste the nicest of all? Poisons can have alarming effects on a person. Could it be possible that all the problems that Dr Abrahamson thought were a result of low blood sugar conditions are actually the result of passive poisoning? Is this why the world is a mad, crazy place? Has this passive poisoning rendered us insane, as well as being visited all manner of horrible afflictions? I don't know, but I do know that I have managed to sort my health problems by cutting out the easily digested high potassium content foods.

With the availability of all kinds of unusual foods, available all year round, how many of us, I wonder, are aware, for instance, that an avocado pear contains three times as much potassium as a banana. A packet of potato crisps contains potato, high in potassium, obviously, and a lot of salt - a food that should be eaten with caution, I should have thought. In Dr Abrahamson's book, he draws attention to mid-afternoon fatigue, chronic fatigue, attacks of extreme weakness, tremulousness, sweating and vertigo. However, these are also symptoms of poisoning. For some reason, this seems to escaped him.

I remember, some years ago, reading an item that stated that cancer was more likely to develop in persons with alkaline systems. Yet, knowing this, a person diagnosed with cancer (as far as I know, and judging by what they eat whilst they are having treatment and "fighting" it), is not asked about their eating habits. And so they carry on, eating the same foods and many of them go on to develop further secondary complications. Some go into "remission" and survive, whilst others go into remission for a while before the disease returns, in a more virulent and fatal form.

Salt and potassium are alkaline. At one time it was thought that they were the same. This, I think was around 1700. I don't have the details to hand unfortunately, but I do recall that it was another hundred years before it was possible to prove the difference by means of electrolysis, which just goes to show how long it can take, to understand just one thing.

Swiftly on... I recall all those years ago when I was on my various diets to stay slim. A breakfast that I would have, would be half a slice of dry toast and a cup of black coffee, without sugar. Then going into Douglas shopping, I would find myself feeling light headed and faint, and would have to sit for a while. I remember once sitting on the staircase, in Marks and Spencer. How many people, I wonder, would have thought that I was drunk, at 11.00 in the morning. Not drunk, but with a very low level of blood sugar. By contrast, I would have some lunch, and after a while would feel lethargic, the wheezing would start. Lunch might have included potatoes, sometimes we had bananas and custard. These are symptoms of poisoning, symptoms of poisoning can start within two and six hours, but the time could be shorter or longer. But that I had symptoms of poisoning would never have occurred to me. Neither, I am sure, would it have occurred to my doctor, and certainly not connected with foods that most of us eat daily.

So, finally. If, I was a doctor, which I am not, the first thing I would want from someone with a problem of some description would be a detailed picture of their diet, with nothing omitted, also what time they ate and what they ate.

There are so many complaints that may be a result of "passive" poisoning. Poisoning can also cause nerve damage. How many people find themselves with problems put down to nerve damage?

What has caused the nerve damage? Truth is stranger than fiction. But it is like a growing thing and eventually finds it's way to the surface.

It is my profound and deep belief that practically all complaints are reversible, cancer, that cancer maybe unfortunate result of a person unwittingly and unknowingly poisoning themselves, causing the body to malfunction, producing all manner of mutant cells. I do believe that our bodies have the most fantastic capacity for recovery, and that given the correct fuel they are capable of restoring perfect balance, without any drugs. Nature is omnipotent.

I believe that we can work with it. If we antagonise it, nature will annihilate us in the end. Perhaps nature's way of ridding the planet of human beings is to gently and slowly render them insensate through passive poisoning.

Chapter 67

I will give some brief idea of what I eat, but a lot of it is common sense. My eating habits now are far removed from Dr Abrahamson's original recommendations. However, I will be eternally in his debt, as it was through his theory that I stumbled on my "accidental knowledge" I am not telling anyone what to do, merely recounting my own experience, and the results achieved.

I disregard the mantra of "five a day" I no longer eat for my palate, but for my continued health. But if I go out for a meal, I enjoy it and then go straight back to my restricted diet, which is, as far as I am concerned, for life. I don't cost the N.H.S a penny, and haven't done for years. Proof of this is to be found on my medical records, then there are the tests conducted more recently at Nobles hospital, Isle of Man.

My staple vegetable foods are onions and celery, and when I can afford them, I also like to include red peppers and mushrooms. I have cut fruit out of my diet, almost altogether. When I do have fruit, I stick to the ones that are low in potassium. The vegetables I eat are low in potassium. I have cut out all root vegetables. I don't consider onions and celery root vegetables. Sometimes I will add some carrot to something I am cooking, but not very often. Everything contains potassium, including meat. How many people know that? I am not including a list of foods and their respective quantities of potassium, since I think it is good for people to do a bit of research on their own behalf. The knowledge that they gain as a result will have more meaning for them.

A useful website to visit for those who are interested is :USDA NATIONAL NUTRIENT DATA BASE for STANDARD REFERENCE; RELEASE 17. Potassium, K (mg) content of selected foods per common measure.

I eat meat every day for my breakfast. Breakfast truly is the most important meal of the day. That is why it is called "breakfast" because the majority will not have eaten for up anything up to fourteen hours. Moreover, it is important to have adequate protein for this first meal of the day, as it is the protein that will keep the blood sugar stable for many hours, whereas a breakfast of cereal will not. A breakfast of cereal is more likely to aggravate chaotic fluctuations in a persons blood sugar, which in turn will be further aggravated by sweet snacks mid-morning, a fast food high carbohydrate lunch, possibly more carbohydrate in the afternoon, rendering the person feeling ragged by the end of the day. In Dr Abrahamson's book, there is an observation, as follows:

"The brain waves of persons with low blood sugar are abnormal. A definite link has been established between low blood sugar as part of a general metabolic imbalance and certain types of insanity" But it may only be a temporary insanity or abnormality, there again, might it last long enough for that person to commit a desperate unthinking crime.

But, what again? What if the established link has been once again misunderstood? And the observed metabolic imbalance, is not as a result of low blood sugar, but as a result of, "passive poisoning". My thoughts drift to, the mad hatters, who were affected by the arsenic used in hat making. What if many acts of violence are committed by people suffering from the effects of "a different form of poisoning", poisoning through sudden unmanageably high levels of potassium, building up in the afternoon onwards. Is it just coincidence, that many violent crimes, are committed in the late afternoon onwards?

Everything contains potassium. I tend to stick to foods that are more slowly digested, thus allowing it to be released into the blood stream more slowly.

Swiftly on....

My breakfasts are straight forward. It can be a chop, or some mince, it is no longer bacon or ham, though I might have some on occasion as a treat. It can even be a roast cooked overnight in my slow cooker. But just to have a simple chop. I cut up an onion and a stick of celery, maybe half a red pepper, if I have one, and put this in an individual casserole dish. To this I add some tomato puree, say about a dessert spoonful, and about a rounded teaspoon of paprika, some soy sauce and coat the chopped vegetables with this. Place the chop on top, or stir in some mince, between 6-8oz. There is no need to add any water whatsoever. A surprising amount of liquid will come out of the meat and the vegetables. Put the lid on the dish, or some foil, and cook for about an hour, not less, can be longer, at 175° C. Whilst it's cooking, I get ready for work. That's it, that's breakfast. A pork chop can be made extra interesting by putting some made up stuffing mix on to the top of the meat, halfway through the cooking. I can get by, at lunchtime, with a drink and some biscuits or a piece of cake. I try not to leave it too late to have my last meal. Sometimes I have two protein meals in a day, sometimes I don't.

If a person has been very ill or debilitated, I would suggest a very gentle introduction to the change of diet. I made a nourishing soup that could be tried. I would suggest that this soup be taken, in small quantities, every half hour, or even every hour, maybe just half a cup full. With small drinks of water in between. I don't take any supplements now, I find that I don't need to.

To make the soup:

Half a mug of quinoa or brown rice, to be added towards the end of the cooking.

Use either a whole chicken, skinned and jointed, or six lamb chops with as much of the fat removed as possible.

Peel and slice four medium sized onions.
Chop a whole head of celery.
Slice two red peppers.
Slice two medium sized carrots (optional)

In a very large saucepan, put enough olive oil to cover the bottom of the pan, and heat until beginning to smoke. To this add the chopped vegetables and prepared meat and lightly fry in the oil.

When the vegetables have softened slightly, add half a small carton of reduced salt marigold vegetable bouillon, stir this in so that it is distributed evenly, then add boiling water to cover the ingredients in the pan. Bring to the boil and simmer until the meat is very tender.

Add the quinoa or rice.

Simmer for another twenty minutes.
Allow to cool.

Remove the meat from the bones and return it to the pan. Discard the bones. Then liquidise the soup.

It is ready to eat, or it can be put in containers and frozen.

It could be made more tasty by the addition of pepper, paprika, tomato puree, or fresh tomatoes during cooking and soy sauce (soy sauce is a salty condiment, but I think, not as harmful, as bacon or ham, I use Organic Tamari, available in Health Food shops). Just add a little of these ingredients at a time until you arrive at a flavour that you like. Easier to add small amounts, than to add too much. If you put too much in, it can't be taken out. Be patient. I wouldn't suggest adding the extra flavouring for someone who is unwell. They need to be coaxed back gently to better health, and should just try persevering with the basic soup for as long as they possibly can. A person who is in relatively good health could have warm rolls with their soup, though it is adequately nutritious with the quinoa. I have a problem with wheat, and on the whole, avoid eating bread. Little scones may be made by beating an egg and adding to that enough rice or buckwheat flour to make a thick batter. Stir in some mixed dried herbs and cook as you would drop scones in a frying pan. They may be eaten with the soup. The soup could be the last meal of the day. A person does not need a heavy meal when they have finished their day's labours. If another meal is required before bed, some porridge is an idea, I make mine with half oats and half ground almonds, made with water. The almonds make it creamy. I stir in some honey or fruit jam e.g. blackcurrant. Out of interest, this is when potassium can be useful, as it will be slowly released from the oats and almonds, and may help a person to feel more relaxed. Sometimes if I've gone to bed a little hungry, rather than be over full, and then find, sometime later, that I really am too hungry to sleep, some porridge and maybe a small cup of warm milk will ensure peaceful sleep.

Sometimes, in the summer, when working days are longer. I may call in to a supermarket and buy some hot cooked meat, which will keep me working until the evening. I can imagine the majority of people saying that they could "never" adopt this life style. As I said earlier, I'm not telling anyone what to do. So that's alright, everyone can carry on as they choose.

Just one last thing,

An alternative recipe for crumble topping:

4oz butter
3oz ground almonds
3oz rice flour
2oz oats
4oz unrefined caster sugar

Blend the rice flour, oats and almonds with the butter and add the sugar, if the mixture seems sticky, add a little more flour and oats.

In an oven proof dish, slice an apple or two depending on the size of the dish used, sprinkle with some sugar and bake at 150° C until crumble topping is browning and juice from the fruit is visible.

About an hour. Another nice filling is blue berries, or apples and plums could be used or just plums. I find it difficult to give quantities as I rarely measure anything.

Chapter 68

I am frequently asked questions about my diet, what have I cut out etc? When I say that it is not just a matter of cutting certain foods out, that there is more to it than that, interest is lost almost immediately. Those that do listen, invariably remark that my diet sounds very boring!

My diet lies somewhere between that of a peasant and a Lord in medieval times 11 – 1400 A.D. Not forgetting, that there are some foods that they ate, which I have cut out and there are some foods that I eat that they didn't.

There are some other considerations that I would like to add, which would be worth mulling over : If I get a cut or a scratch during the course of my work, or if I get a spot, nothing ever becomes infected. If I get an insect bite, there is little or no reaction to it, what little reaction there may be does not progress. In 2011, I was stung by a wasp. The area came up like a blister, perfectly round, about the size of a pound coin. It very slowly decreased, in size, over several months. All that is left now is a very small pink scar.

As I mentioned previously, I am free of winter illness, another winter has just passed, I have not had flu, or a cough, or a sore throat. The only conclusion that I can draw concerning this, is that regarding both bacterial and viral infection, maybe both are attracted to, and thrive in, alkaline saturated systems. By regulating the amount of salt and potassium in my system (the amount of salt that I consume now is negligible), so it is mainly the amount of potassium that is now regulated, which has possibly made me a less attractive host to viruses and bacteria.

Another thing that one should bear in mind, is the amount of cell renewal that is constantly taking place, something that is all too easy to overlook and take for granted. How many of us are aware that the organs that we are born with, are constantly being repaired and renewed, with the exception of our eyes and the most part of our brain.

It was thought that the heart could not renew itself, but as quoted in the Daily Mail October 13th 2009, a study at the New York Medical College found that the heart is actually dotted with stem cells that constantly rejuvenate it.

Prime example : My own heart murmur, which corrected itself.

Other organs are constantly being renewed.

> Lungs – 2-3 weeks
> Taste buds – 10 days
> Liver – 5 months
> Skin – 2-4 weeks
> Intestines – 2-3 days
> Bones – 10 years - another prime example.

Me again : in my twenties I had severe problems with my back (this also whilst I was on a ridiculously poor diet whilst I tried to stay slim). I was referred to a specialist, and told that it was likely that I would need to wear a steel corset by the time that I was 40, and would possibly need to use a wheelchair by the time I was 50. However, when I had a bone density scan at the age of 50, the result showed that my spine was above average density.

> Red blood cells – 4 months.

That information should underline how vitally important it is to have a sound understanding of nutrition. All tissue cells need protein to be ingested, in order to produce new healthy tissue. I have an unshakable belief now, that it also matters what time of day that the protein is eaten.

If a person's diet is high in carbohydrate (which is usually high in potassium) and salt, the body's delicate balance is, at some point, almost guaranteed to fail, in any one of numerous different ways, and a person may become ill. But with one root cause, different people will be affected differently. Also, how much is a poor diet going to affect an unborn child? Pretty drastically, I would say, and a child badly affected by it's mothers diet may have a very difficult life ahead.

If we are taught a better understanding of nutrition and how vitally important well thought out nutrition is, a lot of misery and illness could be avoided. If we understand and accept this fact, then we have only ourselves to blame if we become ill. Moreover, if having become ill, we then drastically modify our diet, we may then have ourselves to thank when we become well again.

People who are against a diet that includes meat, might like to consider ; the following information from *Bartram's Encyclopedia of Herbal Medicine* by Thomas Bartram.

Deficiency of vitamin B12 results in anaemia, loss of appetite, weakness of the nervous system, hearing loss. It is important for mental health. Spina bifida, subacute combined degeneration of the spinal cord.

Also : paranoia, depression mania – even psychosis.

Body effects: healthy nerve tissue, formation of red blood cells.

Sources. All foods of animal origin, meat, liver, kidney, dairy products, cheese, egg yolk, fish, wheatgerm, yeast.

Vitamin B12 cannot be produced in the body and has to be taken up with food. For those who believe that the deficiency can be made up with supplements, I have, in the past, preferred a vegetarian diet, and drifted in and out of that preference for many years. I have tried making up the deficiency with supplements and found them, in my case, not to be to be effective.

Another prime example of how damaging the deficiency of this vitamin can be, is me again, and the very distressing breakdown I had, again, at this time, I was living on a very poor diet, I was given all manner of medication, but there is no nutritional value in drugs, prescribed or otherwise. I am not blaming the doctors, because they did not know. Modern medicine is supposed to perform miracles. But, as I now know, the real miracle is nature itself, and the bodies ability to repair itself. I no longer eat for my palate, I eat to keep my body in healthy working order. It is not a sacrifice. With imagination, there can be lots of variety.

What more can I add?

I've made my case and given what I hope will be some useful advice. All that remains is for me to thank you for reading my story and hope that, in some way, some of you will benefit from my experience.

References

Chapter 45.
Our Own Times 1913-1938 by Stephen King Hall, page 92

Chapter 47.
J. I. Rodale's *Health Treasury*, page 97, 98

Body, Mind and Sugar by Dr. E. M. Abrahdmson and A. W. Pezet, page 99

Chapter 55
Body, Mind and Sugar by Dr. E. M. Abrahdmson and A. W. Pezet, page 114

Chapter 61
Body, Mind and Sugar by Dr. E. M. Abrahdmson and A. W. Pezet, page 126

Chapter 62
Body, Mind and Sugar by Dr. E. M. Abrahdmson and A. W. Pezet, page 127

Chapter 65
Body, Mind and Sugar by Dr. E. M. Abrahdmson and A. W. Pezet, 134, 135

Chapter 66
Body, Mind and Sugar by Dr. E. M. Abrahdmson and A. W. Pezet, page 136

Chapter 67
Body, Mind and Sugar by Dr. E. M. Abrahdmson and A. W. Pezet, page 139

Chapter 68
Bartram's Encyclopedia of Herbal Medicine by Thomas Bartram, page 143, 144